THE
COMPANY
SECRETARY'S
HANDBOOK

THE

COMPANY

SECRETARY'S

HANDBOOK

DAVID V. GIBBONS

FCIS

NEVILLE RUSSELL

Chartered Accountants

CHAPMAN & HALL

University and Professional Division

London · Glasgow · New York · Tokyo · Melbourne · Madras

Published by Chapman & Hall, 2–6 Boundary Row, London SE1 8HN

Chapman & Hall, 2–6 Boundary Row, London SE1 8HN, UK

Chapman & Hall, 2–6 Boundary Row, London SE1 8HN, UK

Blackie Academic & Professional, Wester Cleddens Road, Bishopbriggs, Glasgow G64, 2NZ, UK

Chapman & Hall, 29 West 35th Street, New York NY10001, USA

Chapman & Hall Japan, Thomson Publishing Japan, Hirakawacho Nemoto Building, 6F, 1–7–11 Hirakawa-cho, Chiyoda-ku, Tokyo 102, Japan

Chapman & Hall Australia, Thomas Nelson Australia, 102 Dodds Street, South Melbourne, Victoria 3205, Australia

Chapman & Hall India, R. Seshadri, 32 Second Main Road, CIT East, Madras 600 035, India

First edition 1992

© 1992 Neville Russell Chartered Accountants

Typeset in 11/13pt Bembo by Photoprint, Torquay, Devon
Printed in Great Britain by Richard Clay Ltd, Bungay, Suffolk

ISBN   0 412 45390 8

A catalogue record for this book is available from the British Library

Library of Congress Cataloging-in-Publication data available

CONTENTS

PREFACE

For many years I have been advising secretaries of companies, the majority of whom have been secretaries of private limited companies. Many have been directors' spouses or secretaries and have had no previous knowledge of company matters. It is for them that I have written this book.

Regardless of the size of a company there are basic requirements which all company secretaries have to fulfil or should have the ability to assist their directors in fulfilling. Many changes have occurred in recent years which affect the role and duties of company secretaries and the filing requirements for companies.

It is so easy to blind the reader with science by writing a book in great technical detail. This book has been written so that regardless of what prior knowledge you have you should still be able to ascertain what the requirements might be in a particular situation.

The book is not a legal treatise on the subject of company law and therefore it is only a guide. There may still be times when you will need to refer to the staff at Companies House or your professional advisor. Obviously as a guide and not a treatise on company law, the author, his firm nor the publishers can accept any responsibility for any loss arising from reliance upon the information contained in this book.

I should wish to thank my colleagues at Neville Russell for their encouragement in writing this book, in particular Kim Hurst for her reading of the manuscripts and helpful advice.

For whatever reason you read this book I trust you will find it helpful and informative.

David V. Gibbons
Group Manager
Company Secretarial Services
Neville Russell
Chartered Accountants

INTRODUCTION

Being the secretary of a company means that you are an officer of the company and you have certain responsibilities under the law and under any duties passed to you by the directors.

Within this book you will be able to find help with many of the areas of your responsibility, assisting you to complete the required minutes and making the appropriate returns to Companies House. To help in completing the minutes a number of precedents have been provided in Appendix D which have been cross-referenced to the appropriate part of the text. However, when using any of the precedents you should remember that they are provided solely as a guide and although in the majority of cases they may not need amending, you should always, as a matter of practice, ensure that what the minutes say is true and accurate in all respects.

In the book, references to the 'Act' means the Companies Act 1985 as amended by the Companies Act 1989, and references to sections or schedules mean sections and schedules to that Act.

We will now look at the role, powers and duties of company secretaries.

ROLE

It is a basic requirement that all companies whether public or private must have a company secretary. The Act does not define the role of the company secretary although it does imply that it is administrative rather than managerial. The role of management is that of the directors. As indicated above the secretary is an officer of the company and as such has the duty of ensuring that the affairs of the company are conducted in accordance with:

1. the companies acts;
2. the company's articles; and
3. generally in accordance with the law.

It is for this reason that the directors of public companies are required (section 286) to ensure that the secretary is 'a person who appears to [the directors] to have the requisite knowledge and experience to discharge the function of secretary of the company' and falls within one of five categories listed in that section. The directors, when appointing a secretary for a private company, do not have to meet the requirements of that section but should still appreciate the responsibilities placed upon their company secretary.

POWERS

The company secretary could be described as the chief administrative officer of the company and as such has the authority to enter into contracts on behalf of the company concerning administrative matters. Examples could be contracts relating to staff, office machinery and stationery, hiring of cars and similar matters. But unless the directors give the company secretary specific authority his/her role would not extend to contracts of a managerial nature such as the sale and purchase of goods in which the company deals.

DUTIES

This would vary with the size and nature of the company and the company secretary's terms of employment. Generally speaking the company secretary would attend all meetings, writing up the minutes of such meetings, issue notices to shareholders and others, deal with shareholders' queries regarding transfers and other matters relating to the register of members, be responsible for the books of the company such as the register for members and directors, and for all necessary returns to Companies House. The secretary's duties are not fixed by law but are assigned to him/her by the articles, his/her contract of employment or the directors.

The Act does, however, impose certain responsibilities upon the company secretary. For instance, many of the returns to Companies House, like the annual return, may be signed by either a director or the company secretary. If there is a failure in carrying out a duty of this nature that, such a default could give rise to a liability on the part of the company secretary, when the relevant section imposes a liability upon the officers in default.

These responsibilities may appear onerous but if one works within the framework of the law, which this guide will assist you in doing, you and your directors can avoid the penalties and pitfalls that befall such offices.

1
FORMATION

Let us start at the very beginning by giving an overview of how a company is incorporated and of some of the points to consider — other than commercial ones — when forming a company.

1.1 DOCUMENTATION REQUIRED

The documentation required to form a company is as follows:

1. memorandum and articles of association;
2. form number 10, giving notice of the first directors and the secretary; and
3. form number 12, declaration of compliance;

these must be sent to the Registrar of Companies at Companies House, together with the appropriate registration fee.

1.2 MEMORANDUM OF ASSOCIATION

The memorandum of association states the name of the company; the country within which the registered office will be located (that is either England and Wales, or Scotland); that the company is to be a public company (should that be the case); the objects for which the company is formed or simply that the object of the company is to carry on business as a general commercial company; a statement that the liability of the members is limited; the number of shares and their denomination which would establish the company's initial authorized share capital, and the names and addresses of two persons who propose to take up a specific number of shares (a minimum of one each) on incorporation of the company. The memorandum would then be signed by these two 'subscribers to the memorandum'.

5

1.3 ARTICLES OF ASSOCIATION

The articles regulate the affairs between the shareholders and the management of the company (that is the directors). The Act provides a model set of articles known as Table A. These can be adopted in full, in part or not at all. Where Table A is not adopted at all or only in part, it is necessary for articles to be drawn up covering the required areas of regulation, which would otherwise have been covered by Table A had they not been excluded. Where Table A is not adopted in its entirety the specific articles would need to be signed by the subscribers to the memorandum.

1.4 FORM NUMBER 10

This form sets out, in detail, those persons who consent to become the first directors and the secretary of the company upon its incorporation. The form also states the address of the registered office of the company, again upon incorporation.

1.5 FORM NUMBER 12

Form number 12 declares that the requirements of the Act have been complied with, in regard to the formation of the specific company. The declaration would be completed by one of the directors or the secretary stated in form number 10, or by a solicitor involved in the incorporation of the company.

1.6 NAME

The name of the company is important and the following points should be considered:

1. Is the proposed name too like any other name currently on the Companies Register? This is not only to avoid the name being rejected by the Registrar of Companies but also to reduce the risk of litigation over the use of a particular name by a third party. A check of the trade mark register may also be prudent.
2. Does the proposed name include any word or phrase which requires the consent of a particular department or authority before the Registrar of Companies can accept the name for registration?

1.7 FORMATION AGENTS

One of the simplest ways of setting up a company is to acquire one from a company formation agent. Such an agent would ensure that the name, objects and share capital are as required. However, it can prove more economic to convert what are known as 'off the shelf' companies by carrying out the necessary changes oneself. In saying that, it would probably be advisable not to amend the objects clause without the involvement of a solicitor or other professional, unless it is simply to amend it to a general commercial company (see paragraph 1.2 above).

1.8 MODIFYING PROVISIONS

Precedent P1 provides for the change of name, objects and authorized share capital by way of written resolution. When considering a change of name, the requirements as outlined in paragraph 1.6 above apply equally to a change as they do to selecting a name for incorporation purposes. There is a registration fee which must be paid when submitting the change of name resolution to the registrar.

With regard to increasing the authorized share capital, form 123 needs to be submitted to the Registrar with the specific resolution. For more details with regard to the increase in the authorized share capital please refer to Chapter 3.

1.9 PROBLEMS WITH TWO-MEMBER COMPANIES

Various problems can arise concerning decision-making in a situation where a company has only two members. This can happen either with a 50:50 split of the shares or where there are majority and minority shareholders. A quorum is stipulated by the articles of a company and is usually two members (regulation 40 of Table A). Some articles may provide that a meeting called on the requisition of one of the members (which might occur when there is a dispute) will automatically be dissolved if both members do not attend. In this case, should there be a disagreement between shareholders in a two-member company, all that a minority shareholder needs to do to ensure that the majority shareholder cannot pass a proposed resolution is to fail to attend the meeting. To avoid the need to refer such a matter to the courts for resolution, a mechanism for breaking a deadlock situation should be provided in the articles at the outset.

Under the current Table A, Regulation 41 (concerning proceedings at general meetings), it states that where a quorum is not present at a meeting within half an hour from the appointed time, or if during a meeting such a quorum ceases to be present, the meeting is automatically adjourned to the same day in the following week at the same time and place. That provision may be modified by the addition of the words 'that if at this subsequent meeting the quorum is not present after half an hour, the person or persons present shall constitute a quorum'. Therefore, you could have a quorum of one. When forming a two-member company, consideration should be given to including such a provision at the outset, to avoid difficulties later. An alternative option might be to draw up a shareholders' agreement covering the issue.

1.10 NOTEPAPER

The Act requires certain information about a company to be stated, in legible characters, on its notepaper, namely:

1. the name (even if the company is trading under a different name);
2. the registered office address;
3. the registration number; and
4. the country in which it is registered, i.e. England and Wales, or Scotland.

It is not necessary to state the names of the directors but if they are stated then all the directors' names must appear not just, say, the managing director's.

2

FIRST DIRECTORS' MEETING

Once the company has been formed the directors need to meet to attend to certain matters, in addition to any commercial aspects of the business, which although are of an administrative nature, need to be attended to at the outset.

2.1 THE MINUTES (PRECEDENT P3)

1. Precedent P3 provides a useful guide to the matters which need to be considered following the formation of a company.
2. The precedent is totally flexible and may also be used in conjunction with P1 when changing the name, objects and share capital.
3. A number of the minutes included may not be required at the outset (e.g. appointment of auditors and accounting reference date). The essential matters are the appointment of directors, the issuing of shares and the opening of a bank account. However, it is recommended that as many of the minutes as possible should be included at this stage as they can easily be overlooked at a later date.

2.2 THE MINUTES IN DETAIL

Incorporation of company

---

1. Incorporation of company

It was reported that the company had been incorporated on [date] and the certificate of incorporation numbered [number] together with a print of the memorandum and articles of association in the form in which they were registered with the Registrar of Companies were produced to the meeting.

This is simply to note the fact that the company was duly incorporated.

Directors

2.A First directors

The meeting took formal note that [name] and [name] were appointed the first directors of the Company pursuant to section 13(5), Companies Act 1985.

2.B Appointment of additional directors

It was resolved that [name] and [name] be and are each hereby appointed a Director of the Company. They thereupon took their place at the Meeting as Directors.

2.C Disclosure of interest

In accordance with section 317 of the Companies Act 1985 [name] and [name] each formally disclosed to the Meeting pursuant to Regulations 85 and 86 of Table A in the Companies (Tables A to F) Regulations 1985 his/her interest as a Shareholder and/or Director as follows:

2.D Resignation of directors

There were produced to the Meeting letters addressed to the Company from [name] and from [name] both dated [date] in which they each tendered their resignation as a Director of the Company and in which they each confirmed that they had no outstanding claims against the Company in respect of any matter whatsoever. **It was resolved** ([name] and [name] abstaining from voting on the Resolution) that each resignation be and is hereby accepted. [name] and [name] thereupon ceased to take any further proceedings in the Meeting as Directors.

These minutes provide for most contingencies, including the situation where the new directors are present at the same meeting as the first directors and the first directors are to stand down. Formal letters of resignation will need to be completed by the first directors (precedent P4).

Secretary

3.A First secretary

The Meeting took formal note that [name] had been appointed Secretary of the Company pursuant to section 13(5), Companies Act 1985.

3.B Resignation of secretary

There was produced to the Meeting a letter from [name] to the Company dated [date] containing his resignation as Secretary of the Company and **It was resolved** that his resignation as Secretary be and is hereby accepted.

3.C Appointment of secretary

It was resolved that [name] be and is hereby appointed Secretary of the Company.

This will also only be used in the circumstances indicated in minute 2 above.

Registered office

4.A Registered office

The Meeting took formal note that the Company's registered office pursuant to section 10(6), Companies Act 1985 is at: [address].

4.B Change of registered office

It was resolved that the Company's registered office be and is hereby changed to: [address].

The former is a formal note as to where the registered office was on incorporation. If the registered office is to be changed to another address, the latter would be used (otherwise it should be deleted).

Election of chairman

---

5. Election of chairman

It was resolved ([name] abstaining from voting on the Resolution) that [name] be and is hereby elected Chairman of the Company.

It is advisable to ensure that a chairman is elected at the outset. Most standard forms of articles provide that the chairman has a casting vote at directors' and shareholders' meetings. It is therefore an important appointment. However it is not mandatory to appoint a chairman. In such a case, the minute should be deleted.

Adoption of Seal

---

6. Adoption of Seal

The secretary produced to the Meeting a Seal bearing the Company's name, an impression of which Seal appears in the margin against this resolution, and **It was resolved** that such Seal be and is hereby adopted as the Common Seal of the Company

---

A company is no longer required to have a company seal. However, if a seal is obtained it should be adopted preferably at the first meeting. An advantage of having a seal is that the directors may delegate the witnessing of the seal to persons other than the directors and the secretary. In the absence of a seal, there is no provision for other persons to sign on behalf of the directors and/or secretary.

Appointment of bankers

---

7. Appointment of bankers

It was resolved that [name] of [address] be and is hereby appointed Bankers to the Company in the terms of their Form of Appointment annexed to these Minutes and signed by the Chairman for the purposes of identification **and that** such Form of Appointment be and is hereby deemed to be incorporated in these Minutes except insofar as it has been altered and amended.

If possible, this minute should be completed at the first meeting. A copy of the completed bank mandate form should be annexed to the minutes and signed by the chairman of the meeting. If the bank mandate forms have not been obtained by the date of the meeting, this minute should be deleted and utilized at a later date.

Appointment of auditors

> ### 8. Appointment of auditors
>
> **It was resolved** that Messrs [name], Chartered Accountants of [address] be and are hereby appointed Auditors of the Company pursuant to section 384(2), Companies Act 1985.

If possible, auditors should be appointed at the first meeting. However, it is not mandatory and therefore could be deferred until the business has commenced. Chapter 8 has more information relating to auditors.

Subscriber shares

> ### 9. Subscribers' shares
>
> **It was resolved** that each of the subscribers to the Memorandum of Association be entered in the Registrar of Members as the holder of the Share for which he had agreed to subscribe.

The minute is by way of reminder to enter the subscribers into the register of members, their entry being mandatory under section 22(1).

Transfer of subscriber shares

> ### 10. Transfer of subscribers' shares
>
> There were produced to the Meeting transfers of each of the subscribers' shares as follows:
>
> | TRANSFEROR | NUMBER OF SHARES | TRANSFEREE |
> | --- | --- | --- |
> | [name] | One | [name] |
> | [name] | One | [name] |

It was resolved that the transfers be approved and registered and that the relative Share Certificates be [sealed and] issued to the Transferees.

Unless the two subscribers are to remain as shareholders, the two shares will need to be transferred to new shareholders. If share certificates are not being issued at this stage (e.g. they are to be delayed until a change of name comes through), the relevant words should be deleted.

Allotment of shares

11. Allotment of shares

There were presented to the Meeting applications for shares in the capital of the Company together with cheques covering the subscription monies and **it was resolved** that shares of [value] each of the Company be allotted fully paid to the Applicants whose names are set out in the first column below and so that each Applicant shall receive an allotment of the number of shares specified in the second column below opposite his or her name and that all such shares do rank *pari passu* in all respects.

NAME	NUMBER OF SHARES
[name]	[number]
[name]	[number]
[name]	[number]
[name]	[number]

It was further resolved that Certificates in respect of the shares hereby allotted be [sealed and] issued to the respective allottees.

The minute is drafted to cover those cases where the subscription money is being put up at the meeting. There may be some occasions where the subscription monies are to be paid at some point in the future. In such circumstances the minute will need to be amended to reflect that situation and, perhaps, covering the details as to when calls will be made upon the shareholders to pay for their shares. If the issue of certificates is to be delayed, the relevant words should be deleted. Other amendments may be required to meet the circumstances, particularly if there is going to be a sole allotee. Chapter 3 deals with the issue of shares generally.

Accounting reference date

---

12. Accounting reference date

It was resolved that the accounting reference date of the Company for the purposes of section 224(2), Companies Act 1985 be [date (without year) being the ARD] in each year and that the first set of accounts be prepared for the period from Incorporation of the Company to [date being end of first ARP].

An accounting reference date should if at all possible be elected at the first meeting as, under section 224(2), the initial election of a date must be made within nine months of incorporation. Where no election is made within the specified period, the reference date will be the last day of the month in which the anniversary of the company's incorporation falls (Chapter 4).

Filing of documents

---

13. Filing of documents

The Secretary produced to the Meeting the following returns for filing at the Companies Registry:

a. Forms No. 288 in respect of the changes of Directors and Secretary.
b. Form No. 287 in respect of the change in registered office.
c. Form No. 88(2) in respect of the allotment of shares.
d. Form No. 224 in respect of the accounting reference date.

It was resolved that each form be and is hereby approved **and that** the Secretary be and is hereby authorized and directed to sign each of them on behalf of the Company and arrange for them to be filed at the Companies Registry.

This minute may need to be amended to reflect precisely what forms/documents are to be filed as a consequence of the resolution(s) passed during the meeting.

3

ALLOTMENT OF SHARES

(Including bonus and rights issues)

As we saw in the previous chapter, one of the first events in any company will be the allotment of shares. The purpose of this chapter is to set out in greater detail the whole matter of the issue of shares not only at the outset but also later on in the life of the company and the various terms used.

3.1 DEFINITIONS

For the purposes of this section:

1. An allotment of shares is an allocation of shares to persons who may not previously have been shareholders in the company, e.g. a first allotment of shares (see Chapter 2, minute 11).
2. A bonus issue (sometimes called a scrip issue or a capitalization issue) is the conversion of distributable reserves, or other reserves of the company capable of being capitalized and converted, into paid-up shares.
3. A rights issue is the allotment of shares to existing shareholders in proportion to the number of shares already held by them.
4. An issue may be an allotment, bonus or rights issue.

3.2 BEFORE AN ISSUE

The following matters need to be considered before any issue is made:

1. Whether there is sufficient authorized but unissued share capital available.
2. Whether the directors' authority to allot such unissued shares has expired (see also paragraph 12.6).
3. Whether, in the case of an allotment of shares, the directors have the authority to allot shares otherwise than in proportion to shareholders' existing holdings. This may not be applicable if it is the first issue of shares of the company, other than the two subscriber shares. It is not possible within the scope of this guide to cover every possible situation. Whenever shares are to be issued, therefore, the specific provisions of the articles must be examined.
4. In the case of a rights issue, whether there are any special provisions in the articles relating to such issues where the statutory provisions have been overridden. This will not apply to a public company.
5. In the case of a bonus issue, whether the proposed reserve to be capitalized is capable of being capitalized under the articles. Regulation 110 of Table A enables a company to capitalize profits available for distribution (section 263), share premium account (section 130) and capital redemption reserve (section 170). Not all articles are as wide. Some articles are not specific, e.g. 'out of reserves', but such a phrase would be adequate to cover all three areas. A reference to 'out of the profit and loss account', however, would only cover the use of profits available for distribution.
6. In the case of a bonus issue, whether there are sufficient profits available for distribution to be capitalized. If the last audited financial statements do not show sufficient profits, and the directors are of the opinion that sufficient profits have accumulated since then, the fact that they have considered the latest management accounts, and are of the opinion that sufficient profits do exist, should be minuted.

3.3 THE PRECEDENTS

The resolution to increase the authorized share capital is included in each of precedents P1, P6 and P7. Care should be taken when using the resolution in these precedents to ensure that it does not conflict with the company's articles. The resolution gives the directors wide powers of allotment. The articles may specifically state that any additional shares will be allocated to specific shareholders or a class of shareholders.

For example, the articles may provide that upon the creation of new shares they shall be 'B' shares and be offered before issue to the existing 'B' shareholders. The intention may be to issue 'A' shares to a person not already a member. The resolution increasing the authorized capital creating the new 'A' shares would be in conflict with the articles. Before the resolution may proceed, class meetings will need to be held and the procedure in section 125 (variation of class rights) followed (which principally requires that 75% of the holders of that class must vote in favour, in addition to complying with any relevant provisions in the articles).

The minute in relation to an allotment can be extracted from precedent P3. The minute assumes that the subscription monies have been paid prior to the allotment. If that is not the case, e.g. the allottees are to pay by instalments (known as 'calls'), then the minute will need to be suitably amended. If the shares are to be issued for consideration other than cash, then the minute will need to be amended accordingly. Form 88(2) (allotment for cash or consideration other than cash) will need to be filed within 30 days of the allotment. A form 88(3) may also be required when the consideration is other than cash. Stamp duty may be payable, depending on whether an asset is being transferred to the company.

3.4 BONUS ISSUES

In connection with a bonus issue, precedent P6 should be used with the usual care when using standard documentation. The standard documentation includes a letter of allotment. A form 88(2) will need to be completed. There is no duty payable.

3.5 RIGHTS ISSUES

The precedent for a rights issue is P7 which also includes a letter of allotment. The minutes and allotment letters may need to be amended to meet particular circumstances, e.g. to whom payments are to be made, timing, etc. In most instances the rights issue is for a consideration of cash and therefore form 88(2) will need to be filed within 30 days of the allotment.

3.6 RENUNCIATION

In some instances under both bonus and rights issues the allotments are provisional, giving the holders the right to renounce their bonus or rights to another within a specified time frame. Such facilities avoid the use of the standard transfer form and, particularly with regard to a rights issue, prevents third parties being able to take up shares at a price below the market price. If renunciation does take place stamp duty reserve tax may be payable on the renunciation document.

4

ACCOUNTING REFERENCE DATES AND PERIODS

Again we are to look in more detail at another of the matters that we touched upon when dealing with the first meeting of directors, namely accounting reference dates and periods (see Chapter 2, minute 12).

4.1 DEFINITIONS

An accounting reference date (ARD) is the date in each year to which a company's financial statements are to be prepared, in other words its financial year-end. A company's accounting reference period (ARP) is the period between one ARD and the next, i.e. a company's financial year.

4.2 ELECTION OF AN ACCOUNTING REFERENCE DATE

A company has nine months from the date of incorporation to lodge the required notice (form 224) with the Registrar of Companies electing an ARD. If the company fails to file such a notice within the specified period, its reference date will be the last day of the month in which the anniversary of the company's incorporation falls (unless it was incorporated before 1 April 1990 in which case its reference date will be 31 March).

4.3 CHANGING THE ACCOUNTING REFERENCE DATE

If a company fails to file the required notice in time, or wishes to change its ARD for other reasons, a notice (form 225(1)) may be lodged with the Registrar, before the conclusion of the current ARP, electing a new ARD. If the change is to bring the company's ARD into line with that of its parent or subsidiary undertaking, the company can file the required notice (form 225(2)) after the conclusion of the current ARP, but before the end of the period for filing the financial statements with the Registrar of Companies (see paragraph 4.5 below).

4.4 ACCOUNTING REFERENCE PERIODS

1. The first ARP of the company must run from the date of incorporation to the elected ARD, and must be more than six months but not more than 18 months (section 224(4)).
2. A subsequent ARP may be of any length, provided it does not exceed 18 months. However, an ARP must not exceed 12 months more than once in five years, unless it is to bring the ARD into line with that of a parent or subsidiary undertaking (section 225(4)).
3. Notwithstanding the above, a first ARP can be less than six months if the first ARD is changed to an earlier date as, upon an alteration of the ARD, the minimum period no longer applies. However, for this to be successful it is first necessary to elect an ARD which will provide the company with an ARP of over six months by filing form 224 (see paragraph 4.2 above). During the course of that ARP a form 225(1) may be filed, shortening the ARP to less than six months. The minimum period is set by section 224 and the company complies with it when it files form 224. Section 225 does not set a minimum period and it is within the provisions of that section, upon filing form 225(1), that the company is able to have a first ARP of less than six months.

4.5 FILING PERIODS

The Act sets down strict filing periods, i.e. the period after the end of an ARP within which a company's financial statements must be laid before the members and filed at Companies House. The filing period is ten months for a private company and seven months for a public company (section 244). If a company has overseas connections, the filing period may be extended by three months (section 252) provided notice is given to the Registrar prior to the conclusion of the standard filing period. Annual notice (form 252) is necessary to gain such an extension.

5

ANNUAL GENERAL MEETINGS AND ASSOCIATED MATTERS

Certain events must happen every year whether the company is trading or not. One is the preparation of accounts, another is the holding of an Annual General Meeting (AGM) (although it is now possible for a private company to elect not to hold AGMs following the introduction of the provisions in the Companies Act 1989, as we shall see in paragraphs 12.2 and 12.4), and a third is the filing of an annual return.

5.1 STATUTORY REQUIREMENTS

Companies must hold an AGM in each calendar year unless an elective resolution is in place (see paragraph 12.4). The period between one AGM and the next should not be more than 15 months. A company's first AGM must be held within 18 months from the date of its incorporation and, subject to this, need not be held in the calendar year of its incorporation or in the following year (sections 366, 366A).

The financial statements of a private company must be laid before the members in general meeting and filed with the Registrar of Companies within ten months of its accounting reference date. However, the shareholders of a private company may elect to dispense with the requirement to lay accounts before the members by elective resolution (see paragraph 12.3). A public company's financial statements must be laid before its members and filed with the Registrar of Companies within seven months of its accounting reference date (sections 241, 244). Both filing periods may be extended by three months if the company has some form of overseas connection. Notice on form 252 must be given to the Registrar before the end of the normal filing period in every year in which an extension is claimed (section 252). (Chapter 4 has a more detailed discussion of accounting reference dates and periods.)

If a company's first accounting reference period exceeds 12 months, the filing period is shortened by the number of months by which the 12 month period has been exceeded, subject to a minimum filing period of three months (section 244).

5.2 USE OF STANDARD MINUTES

Precedent P8 covers the directors' approval of financial statements and their receipt by members at the AGM. These provide for the holding of the AGM at short notice. They should, of course, be amended to meet the company's specific requirements.

You may find the following helpful when preparing the minutes:

1. Ascertain who is to sign the balance sheet.
2. Check the articles to see if rotation of directors applies. This is where a proportion of the directors, usually one-third, are required to retire at each AGM. Care should be taken as the rules in Table A do not always apply, e.g. some companies have life directors who are not to be included in determining the number who should retire by rotation.
3. If rotation applies, check the previous years' minutes to identify who should retire in the current year and any directors who have been appointed during the year, as they too may need to retire at the AGM. (If the financial statements are being presented to an extraordinary general meeting, rotation will not apply.)
4. Check the Articles to see whether the reappointment of auditors may be dealt with as ordinary business. (Note that private companies may elect to dispense with the annual appointment of auditors, see paragraph 12.5.)

5.3 ADJOURNING THE AGM

Sometimes the financial statements may not be available in time for the due date of the AGM. This should be ascertained at least one month before the due date. It is still necessary to hold the AGM by the due date, but it can be adjourned until such time as the financial statements are available. If the company has overseas connections, this would allow time for the client to notify the Registrar that an extended filing period is being claimed (see section 4.5). The precedent is P10.

5.4 RECONVENING THE AGM

Upon the financial statements becoming available use precedent P11.

5.5 THE ANNUAL RETURN

A company's annual return (form A363) is required to be made up to a date not later than its 'return date' and filed at Companies House within 28 days of the date to which it is made up. A company's 'return date' is the anniversary of the date to which its previous return was made up or, if there was no previous return, the anniversary of the company's incorporation. The return must be signed by a director or the secretary of the company (section 363).

Companies House will send to each company the required form about one month prior to the return date. The form will contain such information as is currently held on the computer at Companies House. Therefore it will only be necessary to check the information (adding any information that may be required), sign the form and return it to Companies House with the required filing fee within the timetable indicated above.

6

NOTICE PERIODS
AND MEETINGS
GENERALLY

During the life of the company meetings must be held, whether they are directors' meetings to enable the directors to manage and direct the business, or shareholders' meetings. The purpose of this chapter is to give an overview of such meetings and the notice periods required to convene them.

6.1 SHAREHOLDERS' MEETINGS

There are three types of shareholders' meetings namely annual general meetings, extraordinary general meetings and class meetings.

6.2 NOTICE PERIODS FOR SHAREHOLDERS' MEETINGS

The notice period required for a specific shareholders' meeting is dependent upon the type of meeting and/or the business to be conducted at the meeting. Basically there are two periods as follows:

1. Twenty-one days' notice for Annual General Meetings and for Extraordinary General Meetings and class meetings (if a special resolution is to be proposed at such a meeting).
2. Fourteen days' notice for Extraordinary General Meetings and class meetings (except where a special resolution is being proposed at that meeting).

6.3 CLEAR DAYS

When calculating the number of days notice, reference should be made to the articles of association as to whether the number of days are 'clear days' or not. Regulation 38 of Table A specifies that the number of days should be clear days, that is excluding the date of service (48 hours after posting, see regulation 115) and the date of the meeting. It can be seen, therefore, that the 21 days' notice for an Annual General Meeting could in fact be as many as 25 days. The articles of the company would give further guidance with regard to the giving of notice, for instance Regulation 112 of Table A provides that notice should only be sent to the first name and address where there are joint holders of shares. Also if a non-United Kingdom member doesn't give to the company an address within the United Kingdom at which notices can be served, such a member shall not be entitled to notice.

6.4 TYPES OF RESOLUTIONS

There are four different types of resolutions that can be proposed at a meeting of shareholders and each has its own majority by which the resolution is deemed to have been passed, as follows:

1. ordinary resolution: simple majority;
2. extraordinary resolution: 75% majority;
3. special resolution: 75% majority;
4. elective resolution: 100% majority.

Written resolutions (see paragraph 12.1) must be signed by all members entitled to attend and vote except a written resolution in lieu of a class meeting where not less than 75% in nominal value of the shares of the relevant class need sign (see section 125).

6.5 QUORUM

A shareholders' meeting cannot commence until a quorum is present, that is, a minimum number of shareholders. The articles would state the number who would represent a quorum, for instance, Regulation 40 of Table A provides that 'two persons entitled to vote upon the business to be transacted, each being a member or a proxy for a member or a duly authorized representative of a corporation, shall be a quorum'. That quorum should be maintained throughout the course of the meeting.

6.6 VOTING

Voting on a resolution would initially be by show of hands when each shareholder present in person (not by proxy) would be entitled to one vote. If a poll is taken, votes would be by reference to the number of shares held and would also include votes by proxy holders.

Who may ask ('demand') for a poll to be taken would be set out in the company's articles. For example, regulation 46 of Table A provides that 'a poll may be demanded by

1. the chairman; or
2. at least two members having the right to vote at the meeting; or
3. a member or members representing not less than one-tenth of the total voting rights of all the members having the right to vote at the meeting; or
4. a member or members holding shares conferring the right to vote at the meeting, being shares on which an aggregate sum has been paid up equal to not less than one-tenth of the total sum paid up on all the shares conferring the right'.

A proxy can join in the demand for a poll.

Where there is an equality of votes a chairman may have a second or casting vote subject to the articles (see Chapter 2, minute 5).

6.7 NOTICE PERIODS FOR DIRECTORS' MEETINGS

As neither the Act nor Table A lays down a notice period for directors' meetings, some company's articles add a provision laying down a specific notice period. In the majority of cases, regulation 88 of Table A applies; this says 'the directors may regulate their proceedings as they think fit'. If that regulation applies, the directors should be advised to lay down what notice period should be given for directors' meetings failing which 'reasonable' notice should be given. Notice of a directors' meeting need not be in writing (regulation 111 of Table A) unless the articles provide otherwise. Likewise notice need not be given to a director out of the United Kingdom (regulation 88) unless the articles provide otherwise.

6.8 QUORUM

As with shareholders' meetings, a quorum must be present before the business of the board of directors may proceed. Regulation 89 of Table A provides that the quorum 'may be fixed by the directors and unless so fixed as the quorum at any other number, shall be two'.

6.9 MINUTES

It is a requirement of the Act (section 382) that minutes of the proceedings of all shareholders' and directors' meetings be recorded in suitable books which must be maintained and kept throughout the life of the company. Shareholders have the right to inspect the minutes of shareholders' meetings (section 383) but not those of the directors, which are only available to the directors and the auditors.

6.10 SPECIAL NOTICE

Special notice is notice given to a company by a member, to the effect that he/she is to propose the resolution contained in that notice, at least 28 days before the meeting at which the resolution is to be proposed. Special notice should not be confused with special resolutions (section 379(1)).

7

THE DIRECTORS AND THE SECRETARY

We saw how the first directors and the secretary were appointed when looking at formation (Chapter 1), and briefly covered their resignation and appointment of others when looking at the first directors' meeting (Chapter 2). Here we shall look at the whole subject in a little more depth.

7.1 APPOINTMENT OF DIRECTORS

First directors

Upon the incorporation of a company, those persons who were named in the documents (Form 10) lodged with Companies House as having consented to act, shall be the first directors (section 13(5)).

Subsequent directors

Generally the directors for the time being of a company have the power to appoint additional directors (see regulation 78 of Table A). However, the following should be noted:

1. The shareholders may appoint directors either in general meeting or (if it is a private company) by written resolution (see paragraph 12.1).
2. The number fixed by the articles as the maximum number of directors should not be exceeded (not all articles limit the number of directors).
3. The articles should be examined to see whether any shareholding qualification is required (this is very rare nowadays but refer to

section 291 if it does) or for other specific requirements and/or restrictions (see below).

4. The need to obtain the person's consent to becoming a director as required by section 288 (form 288).

If the current directors are to appoint additional directors the wording of an appropriate minute can be found in minute 2B of the first directors' meeting precedent (see paragraph 2.1).

In some instances a shareholder or class of shareholder may have the right to appoint one or more persons as directors of a company. In such cases the specific requirements of the articles should be followed, normally the lodging of a written notice at the company's registered office is all that is required (see also 7.4).

Form 288 once signed by the appointee consenting to act, should be countersigned by either another director or the secretary, after which (within 14 days of the date of appointment) it should be filed at Companies House.

7.2 REGISTER OF DIRECTORS

The relevant particulars (the same information as contained in form 288) are to be entered in the register of directors. The following points should be noted for the purposes both of completing the form and entering details in the register of directors:

1. Name: this means full name (John H Smith, for example, is not sufficient).
2. Former Name: a married woman's maiden name is not required.
3. Address: this means the person's residential address, not his/her office address or his/her company's address.
4. Date of birth: this is required regardless of the status of the company.
5. Nationality
6. Occupation: try and avoid the term 'company director' as that by itself is meaningless.

When recording 'other directorships' remember to include all directorships held over the past five years. A company that has gone into liquidation is still a 'live' directorship until the conclusion of the winding up process. Directorships in respect of the following may be excluded:

1. dormant companies (if they have been dormant throughout the directorship);
2. a holding company of which the company making the return is a wholly-owned subsidiary;
3. a wholly-owned subsidiary of the company making the return;
4. any other wholly-owned subsidiary of the same holding company.

7.3 LEAVING OFFICE

Resignation

Regulation 81(d) of Table A provides that a director may resign from his office as director. The lodgement of the letter at the registered office or with the chairman or secretary is all that is required. The resignation letter comes into effect from the date of lodgement and not from any subsequent board meeting when the resignation is accepted or noted.

Rotation

Regulation 73 of Table A provides for the rotation of directors, i.e. the standing down of one-third of the board at each successive annual general meeting. Where a director comes up for rotation he/she may simply advise the company that he/she does not wish to stand again or, if he/she does stand again, the motion to re-elect him/her may be lost. In both cases he/she would cease to be a director with effect from the conclusion of the annual general meeting. If a company has elected not to hold annual general meetings, rotation would cease to have effect.

Removal

A director may be removed from office at any time by passing an ordinary resolution to that effect (section 303). A director whose removal is proposed may make representations to the members and speak at the meeting at which the resolution to remove him/her is considered. A director may not be removed by a written resolution (see paragraph 12.1).

Special notice (see paragraph 6.10) must be given of the proposed resolution, a copy of which must be sent to the director concerned by the company upon its receipt. The giving of special notice does not oblige the directors to convene a general meeting to consider the motion or to include it in the notice of the next annual general meeting. It may be necessary, therefore, for the shareholders simultaneously to request a general meeting under section 368 to consider the resolution.

Some articles provide that, notwithstanding section 303, a director may be removed by extraordinary resolution. The advantage is that special notice is not required and therefore the meeting can be convened on 14 days' notice (special notice requires 28 days). However, a 75% majority of those voting is required instead of a simple majority.

General

Special provisions often exist in subsidiary company articles or joint venture articles or where a specific shareholder has the right to be represented on the board of directors. The effect of such provisions is to enable a particular shareholder or shareholders to appoint or remove one or more directors by written notice to the company.

Upon a director ceasing to act, for whatever reason, form 288 is required to be filed at Companies House within 14 days and the relevant entries made in the register of directors.

7.4 CATEGORIES OF DIRECTOR

Under company legislation, a person either is or is not a director. However, adjectives are sometimes added to describe a specific function or role. The more common ones are examined below.

Managing director

The member of the board to whom the management of the day-to-day operations of the company has been delegated (sometimes referred to as the chief executive).

Executive director

A salaried director of the company having a specific functional responsibility delegated by the board, e.g. finance director, sales director, etc. (including the managing director).

Non–executive director

Any director other than an executive director. (Normally they just attend the board meetings of the company.) The responsibilities and duties to the company are no less onerous that those of an executive director.

Nominee director

A director appointed by a specific shareholder (see paragraphs 7.1 and 7.3). Although nominated by a shareholder, like any other director his/her responsibilities and duties are to the company as a whole.

Alternate director

If a company's articles so provide (see regulations 65 and 69 of Table A), a director who is unable to attend board meetings may appoint another person to attend in his/her place. If the person appointed is not already a director of the company, form 288 will need to be completed and filed. An alternate director is not an agent of his/her appointor and is responsible for his/her own acts and/or omissions.

Shadow director

A person who, although not a director, influences the way the actual directors manage the company. A shadow director is defined by the Act as 'a person in accordance with whose directions or instructions the directors of the company are accustomed to act' (section 741(2)). A person is not deemed a shadow director, however, by virtue of the directors acting on advice given by him/her in a professional capacity. Form 288 is required to be filed for a shadow director and his/her particulars recorded in the register of directors (section 288(6)).

7.5 COMPANY SECRETARY

We saw in the introduction that every company is required to have a secretary and touched upon his/her role and duties. Here we cover the matter of his/her appointment and demission. It should be noted that a sole director may not also be the secretary.

7.6 APPOINTMENT OF THE SECRETARY

The first secretary of the company is the person named as secretary in the statement (Form 10) lodged at Companies House with the other formation documents (section 13(5)). Subsequent appointments may be made by the directors in accordance with the articles of association (for example, regulation 99 of Table A).

7.7 LEAVING OFFICE

A secretary may resign from office. The directors may remove a person from the office of secretary at any time in accordance with the articles of association. Such removal would be without prejudice to the terms and conditions of the individual's contract of service.

7.8 REGISTRATION OF THE SECRETARY

Upon any change of secretary or his/her particulars, the Registrar must be notified within 14 days on form 288 and the relevant entries made in the register of directors and secretaries.

8

AUDITORS: APPOINTMENT, REMOVAL AND RESIGNATION

We saw in looking at the first directors' meeting that one of the matters for consideration was the appointment of auditors. In this chapter we will look at their appointment, etc. in more detail.

8.1 APPOINTMENT OF AUDITORS

Every company, other than a dormant company (see paragraph 16.2), is required to appoint auditors (section 384(1)).

All companies (except private companies which have elected to dispense with the laying of accounts (see paragraph 12.3) shall appoint auditors at each general meeting at which accounts are laid, normally the company's Annual General Meeting (section 385(2)).

In practice the auditors will normally be appointed at the first directors' meeting (see Chapter 2, minute 8). However, provided the auditors are appointed prior to the first general meeting of the company at which accounts are laid, there is no specific date by which they should be appointed. If the directors fail to make an appointment, the members may appoint the first auditors in general meeting (section 385(3), (4)). The company must, of course, bear in mind the timetable for laying audited accounts before the members (see paragraph 4.5).

Where a private company has elected to dispense with the laying of accounts (see paragraph 12.3; section 385A(1)) the rules differ as follows:

1. Initially the directors shall appoint the first auditors of the company at any time before:
   (a) 28 days after the date copies of the first annual accounts are sent to members; or
   (b) if notice requiring the accounts to be laid before a general meeting is given, the beginning of that meeting (section 385A (3), (4)).
2. Annually the company should appoint auditors in general meeting within 28 days of the date copies of the annual accounts for the previous financial year are sent to members (or, if notice requiring the accounts to be laid before a general meeting is given, before the conclusion of that meeting) (section 385A(2)). However, in practice, where a private company has elected not to lay accounts before the members in general meeting it also elects not to reappoint auditors annually, thus avoiding the above procedures.

8.2 ELECTION BY PRIVATE COMPANY TO DISPENSE WITH ANNUAL APPOINTMENT

As indicated above a private company may elect to dispense with the annual appointment of auditors (section 386(1)). Where such an election is in force, the company's auditors shall be deemed to be reappointed automatically on the expiry of the time allowed for appointing auditors unless:

1. a resolution to bring their appointment to an end has been passed (see paragraph 8.6); or
2. in the case of a dormant company, a resolution has been passed by such a company to be exempt from the obligation to appoint auditors (section 386(2)).

8.3 APPOINTMENT BY SECRETARY OF STATE

If no auditors are appointed, reappointed or deemed to be re-appointed before the end of the time allowed for appointing auditors, the Secretary of State may appoint a person to fill the vacancy. The company is required to notify the Secretary of State within one week of the end of the time allowed for appointing auditors of his power having become exercisable (section 387).

8.4 CASUAL VACANCIES

Casual vacancies may arise in the following circumstances:

1. the death of the auditor;
2. the resignation of the auditor; or
3. the removal of the auditor during his/her term of office.

The directors, or the company in general meeting, may appoint an auditor to fill any casual vacancy. If the members are to fill the vacancy, special notice (see paragraph 6.10) of the resolution will be required (section 388(1), (3)). Where an auditor has been appointed by the directors to fill a casual vacancy, special notice is required for a resolution at a general meeting to reappoint him/her. The former auditor, if he/she resigned, is entitled to receive a copy of the notice (section 388(3), (4)).

If there were joint auditors, the surviving auditor may continue to act until such time as the vacancy is filled (section 388(2)).

8.5 JOINT AUDITORS

If joint auditors are to be appointed from the outset, paragraph 8.2 above applies (appointment to be made by the directors or, failing that, the members). In any other case the Act is silent. The appointment of a joint auditor, i.e. another firm to act alongside the current auditor, would not be the filling of a casual vacancy and therefore special notice should be given of the resolution (a copy to be forwarded to the retiring auditor) (section 391(1), (2)).

A surviving auditor may continue to act until any vacancy is filled but such a vacancy need not be filled unless there is a specific requirement for the company to have joint auditors.

8.6 AUDITOR REMOVED OR NOT REAPPOINTED

A company may remove an auditor from office at any time by passing an ordinary resolution to that effect. Where such a resolution is passed, the company must notify the registrar within 14 days. Notwithstanding his/her removal, the auditor has the right to receive notice of, attend and be heard at any general meeting of the company:

1. at which his/her term of office would otherwise have expired (i.e. at the next annual general meeting); or
2. at which it is proposed to fill the vacancy caused by his/her removal; this would only occur if the directors do not fill the vacancy (see paragraph 8.4 above) (section 391(1), (2), (4)).

An auditor cannot be removed by a written resolution signed by all the members (paragraph 1(b) of Schedule 15A to the Act; see paragraph 12.1).

Special notice (see paragraph 6.10 and paragraph 8.10) is required for a resolution removing an auditor before the end of his/her term of office or appointing as auditor a person other than the retiring auditor. On receipt of such notice, the company must send a copy of it to the auditor proposed to be removed or to the auditor proposed to be appointed and to the retiring auditor (section 391A(1), (2)).

The auditor whose removal is proposed, or the retiring auditor, has a right to have written representations circulated to the members. If they are received too late for circulation prior to the meeting (or the company fails to circulate them), the auditor may require them to be read out at the meeting (section 391A(3), (4), (5)).

The auditor's representations need not be circulated, or read out at the meeting, if the company or any other person claiming to be aggrieved satisfies the court that the auditor is abusing his/her rights to secure needless publicity for defamatory matter. The auditor may be ordered to pay all or part of the company's costs in connection with such an application (section 391A(6)).

8.7 AUDITOR RESIGNS

An auditor may resign from office by submitting a letter of resignation to the company at its registered office. The letter must be accompanied by a statement of any circumstances connected with his/her resignation which the auditor considers should be brought to the attention of the members or creditors of the company (or a statement that there are no such circumstances) (section 392(1)).

An auditor's resignation takes effect on the date his/her letter is received at the company's registered office or on such later date as is specified in the letter. The company must send a copy of the auditor's letter of resignation to Companies House within 14 days of its receipt (section 392(2), (3)).

Where the auditor's letter of resignation is accompanied by a statement of circumstances which he/she considers should be brought to the attention of the members or creditors, he/she (the auditor) may requisition an extraordinary general meeting (EGM). The directors must then convene a meeting within 21 days for a date not more than 28 days after the date of the notice convening the meeting (section 392A(1), (2), (5)).

Notwithstanding his/her resignation, the auditor has the right to receive notice of, attend and be heard at:

1. a meeting convened on his/her requisition; or
2. any general meeting at which his/her term of office would otherwise have expired, e.g. the next annual general meeting.

He/she also has the right to have a written statement of the circumstances connected with his/her resignation circulated to the members. If the statement is received too late for circulation prior to the meeting (or the company fails to circulate it), the auditor may require it to be read out at the meeting (section 392A(3), (6), (8)).

The auditor's statement need not be circulated, or read out at the meeting, if the company or any other person claiming to be aggrieved satisfies the court that the auditor is abusing his/her rights to secure needless publicity for defamatory matter. The auditor may be ordered to pay all or part of the company's costs in connection with such an application (section 392A(7)).

8.8 TERMINATION OF APPOINTMENT OF AUDITORS NOT APPOINTED ANNUALLY

Where a private company has elected to dispense with the annual appointment of auditors, any member may give written notice to the company at its registered office proposing that their appointment be brought to an end. The directors must then convene a meeting of the company (normally an extraordinary general meeting) to vote on the matter. The date of the meeting should not be more than 28 days after the date the notice was given. If the directors fail to convene a meeting within 14 days, the member concerned may himself convene the meeting (section 393(1), (2), (4)).

If the meeting decides that the auditors' appointment should be brought to an end the actual date of cessation would be:

1. the date they would otherwise have been deemed to be reappointed; or

2. if the notice was given by the member within 14 days of the date the annual accounts were sent to members, immediately (section 393(3)).

8.9 STATEMENT BY AUDITOR CEASING TO HOLD OFFICE

An auditor who ceases to hold office (for whatever reason) is required to submit a statement to the company's registered office of any circumstances connected with his/her ceasing to hold office which he/she considers should be brought to the attention of the members or creditors (or a statement that there are no such circumstances) (section 394(1)).

Where the auditor resigns, the statement must be submitted along with his/her notice of resignation (see paragraph 8.7 above). Where the auditor does not seek reappointment, the statement must be submitted not less than 14 days before the end of the time allowed for next appointing auditors. In any other case, the statement must be submitted not later than 14 days after the date on which the auditor ceases to hold office (section 394(2)).

The company need not circulate the statement to members if it satisfies the court that the auditor is using the statement to secure needless publicity for defamatory matter. The auditor may be ordered to pay all or part of the company's costs in connection with such an application (section 394(6)).

If the company does not apply to the court, the statement must be sent, within 14 days of receipt, to every person entitled to receive copies of the annual accounts. If the auditor is not notified of an application to the court within 21 days of submitting the statement, he/she must send a copy to the Registrar within a further seven days (section 394(3)–(5)).

8.10 SPECIAL NOTICE

Special notice (see paragraph 6.10) is required when a resolution is to be proposed at a general meeting to:

1. appoint as auditor a person other than the retiring auditor (see paragraph 8.8);
2. fill a casual vacancy (see paragraph 8.4 above);
3. reappoint a retiring auditor who was appointed by the directors to fill a casual vacancy (see paragraph 8.4 above); or

4. remove an auditor before the end of his/her term of office (see paragraph 8.6 above).

8.11 AUDITORS' REMUNERATION

The auditors' remuneration is to be determined in the following manner:

1. If the auditor was appointed by the directors or the Secretary of State, they shall determine the remuneration.
2. In any other case, the company in general meeting shall determine the remuneration or the manner in which it is to be determined (e.g. the meeting authorizes the directors to determine the remuneration) (section 390A(1), (2)).

9

DIVIDENDS

One of the goals of the management of a company should be the payment of a dividend to the shareholders. They have risked their money by investing in the company and therefore should receive some reward. Of course that does not always follow where the directors and the shareholders are the same. The directors may therefore receive their reward by way of a salary and other benefits, although that would not exclude them from receiving a dividend in addition, if profits allow.

9.1 CATEGORIES OF DIVIDEND

The payment of a dividend may fall within the following categories:

1. an interim dividend payable on ordinary or unclassified shares (i.e. those not having a fixed coupon) during the course of an accounting period;
2. a final dividend as in 1 above payable upon the completion of the statutory accounts for the relevant accounting period;
3. a fixed dividend in accordance with the terms of issue and/or articles;
4. a participating dividend which is paid in addition to a fixed dividend if the terms of issue and/or the articles so provide.

This chapter is principally concerned with the payment of dividends under 1 and 2 above.

9.2 PROFITS BEFORE DIVIDENDS

Regardless of which category a dividend falls within, it is unlawful for a company to pay a dividend unless it has sufficient distributable profits for the purpose. The amount which is distributable is the company's accumulated realized profits (not previously distributed or capitalized) less its accumulated realized losses (not previously written off), with additional requirements for public and investment companies (section 263(3)).

In considering whether it is lawful to pay an interim dividend, the directors would first refer to the last set of statutory accounts and also need to consider the impact if the audit report on those accounts was qualified in any way. If there were insufficient distributable reserves by reference to those accounts, reference should be made to up-to-date management accounts and properly prepared projections for the remainder of the current accounting period. This is a procedure which any prudent director would reasonably be expected to follow to enable him/her to assess not only whether the company has sufficient distributable reserves available but also whether payment of the dividend would adversely affect the company's financial position during the remainder of the accounting period (sections 270 & 271). A public company is required to produce interim accounts in accordance with section 272.

If there were sufficient distributable reserves by reference to the last set of statutory accounts but the audit report on those accounts was 'qualified', a dividend cannot be paid unless the auditor states in writing that in his/her opinion the payment of a dividend would not contravene section 263 and that statement has been laid before the members in general meeting (section 271).

If a company has not prepared its first set of statutory accounts, reference would need to be made to management accounts as above. A public company would need to prepare and file initial accounts in accordance with section 273.

9.3 WHO DECLARES?

The articles of a company normally provide (see regulations 102 and 103 of Table A) that the directors may declare an interim dividend and the shareholders a final dividend. The final dividend cannot exceed the amount recommended by the directors.

9.4 THE MINUTES

Precedents P18 and P19 call for three dates:

1. the date of the meeting, which would also be the date the dividend is declared;

2. the cut-off date for those appearing in the register of members as being entitled to receive the dividend (effectively the date the shares become ex-dividend); and
3. the payment date being the date on which the dividend is to be paid (which can be the same day as the meeting or a later date).

Upon the payment of a dividend, form CT61 would need to be completed and the relevant amount of advance corporation tax paid over to the Collector of Taxes.

A final dividend is normally declared at the company's annual general meeting. If a private company has elected not to hold annual general meetings (see paragraph 12.4), such a dividend could be declared by written resolution or at an extraordinary general meeting. The use of the terms 'interim' and 'final' are not restrictive in that a company may declare more than one interim dividend and no final or more than one final dividend.

9.5 WAIVER OF DIVIDEND

A shareholder may waive his/her right to receive a dividend by deed lodged with the company prior to the dividend being declared.

10

TRANSFER OF SHARES

We touched very briefly on the matter of the transfer of shares when dealing with the first directors' meeting (Chapter 2, minute 10). Here we will go into the matter in more depth as in any company, large or small, share transfers will need to take place at some time or other.

10.1 BASIC REQUIREMENTS

The following are the basic requirements to effect a valid transfer of shares:

1. A duly signed stock transfer form stamped with the appropriate amount of stamp duty, or exempted from stamp duty.
2. The share certificates relating to the shares to be transferred must be surrendered to the company or, if lost or destroyed, an indemnity duly completed by the transferor.
3. In the case of unquoted companies, a resolution of the directors approving the transfer.

10.2 REGISTERING THE TRANSFER

When registering the transfer in the statutory books (principally the register of members) of the company, it is essential that the date appearing in the register of members does not precede the date of the transfer, the date the stamp duty was paid and the date of the minute.

10.3 CHECK THE ARTICLES

Care should be taken to ensure that the proposed transfer does not conflict with the articles. Pre-emption rights may exist. If all the other shareholders are content that the share transfer should take place, notwithstanding that it is contrary to the articles, a special resolution or preferably written resolution signed by all the shareholders should be passed before the transfer is approved and registered. Always check the articles as an alternative procedure may be provided.

10.4 DEATH OF A SHAREHOLDER

Where a joint shareholder dies, the death certificate is all that is required to delete the deceased from the register, leaving the remaining joint holder or holders as the holder(s) of those shares.

If a single shareholder dies, an office copy of probate or letters of administration would be needed, or such other evidence as may be appropriate in the circumstances to ensure that the person or persons completing the transfer, e.g. the executors, can validly do so.

11

STAMP AND CAPITAL DUTY

In paragraph 10.2 it was noted that any transfer form presented to the company for registration should be stamped. This chapter will look at stamp duty (solely as it applies to the transfer of shares) a little closer. However you should note that Section 108 of the Finance Act 1990 provided for the abolition of stamp duty on the transfer of shares. At the time of going to press that provision had not yet been brought into effect.

11.1 RATE

The standard rate of stamp duty is 50p per £100 of consideration or part of £100.

11.2 EXEMPT TRANSACTIONS

Certain transactions are totally exempt from duty which are listed on the reverse of standard stock transfer forms. Such transactions include:

1. The transfer of shares into the names of trustees of a trust and between trustees on the retirement and/or appointment of new trustees.
2. The transfer of shares to the beneficiary named in a will (or his/her nominee).
3. Transfers in connection with divorce.
4. The transfer by the liquidator of shares which formed part of the assets of the company in liquidation to a shareholder of that

company (or his/her nominee) forming part of his rights on a winding–up.

5. Transfers by way of gift.

For the transfer forms to be accepted by the company or its registrars the following certificate must be completed on the reverse of the transfer form (most transfer forms now have the certificate already printed on the reverse):

> I/We hereby certify that this instrument falls within category . . . in the Schedule to the Stamp Duty (Exempt Instruments) Regulations 1987.

The certificate should be signed by the transferor or grantor or by his/her solicitor or duly authorized agent. A solicitor may sign in the name of his/her firm. The term 'duly authorized agent' includes a licensed conveyancer as well as a banker, stockbroker or accountant, etc. Where the certificate is not signed by the transferor, grantor or his/her solicitor, it must contain a statement by the signatory of the capacity in which he/she signs, that he/she is authorized so to sign and that he/she gives the certificate from his/her own knowledge of the facts stated in it.

11.3 TAKEOVERS

In addition to the above, stamp duty is not payable where one company acquires all the shares of another, provided the following provisions of the Finance Act 1986 are all met:

1. The registered office of the acquiring company is in the United Kingdom.
2. The transfer forms part of an arrangement by which the acquiring company acquires the whole of the issued share capital of the target company.
3. The acquisition is effected for bona fide commercial reasons and does not form part of a scheme or arrangement of which the main purpose, or one of the main purposes, is avoidance of liability to stamp duty, stamp duty reserve tax, income tax, corporation tax or capital gains tax.

4. The consideration for the acquisition consists only of the issue of shares in the acquiring company to the shareholders of the target company.
5. After the acquisition has been made, each person who immediately before it was made was a shareholder of the target company is a shareholder of the acquiring company.
6. After the acquisition has been made, the shares in the acquiring company are of the same classes as were the shares in the target company immediately before the acquisition was made.
7. After the acquisition has been made, the number of shares of any particular class in the acquiring company bears to all the shares in that company the same proportion as the number of shares of that class in the target company bore to all the shares in that company immediately before the acquisition was made.
8. After the acquisition has been made, the proportion of shares of any particular class in the acquiring company held by any particular shareholder is the same as the proportion of shares of that class in the target company held by him/her immediately before the acquisition was made.

The above exemption has very little scope now in company reorganizations.

11.4 REPURCHASE OF SHARES

Stamp duty at the standard rate is also payable on any repurchase by a company of its own shares. The duty is payable on the return which has to made to the Registrar of Companies (Form 169) (see paragraph 14.1).

11.5 INTRA-GROUP TRANSFERS

A transfer of shares from one company to another in the same group (holding at least 90% of the other) is still exempt from stamp duty provided:

1. the consideration is received (directly or indirectly) by a group company (i.e. not a third party who is not a group company);
2. the interest was transferred (directly or indirectly) to a person as in 1; or
3. the 'group' relationship between the transferor and transferee was not to cease.

11.6 FIXED DUTY TRANSACTIONS

Although under paragraph 11.2 above total exemption from duty is provided (where property is transferred otherwise than on sale) there are still some cases where duty is not relieved. Examples are:

1. transfer from a beneficial owner to his/her nominee;
2. transfer from a nominee to the beneficial owner;
3. transfer from one nominee to another nominee of the same beneficial owner;
4. transfer by way of security for a loan or retransfer to the original transferor on repayment of a loan;
5. transfer from the trustrees of a profit sharing scheme to a participant in the scheme.

Transfers within these categories and others not appearing in paragraph 11.2 above should be presented to a stamp office in the normal way. The certificate on the reverse of the transfer form will need completing. Some documents that do not operate to convey any interest in property remain liable to 50p fixed duty, e.g. declaration of trust, divided waiver and surrender. These too should be presented to a stamp office in the normal way.

11.7 CAPITAL DUTY

Capital duty is no longer payable.

12

THE ELECTIVE
REGIME FOR PRIVATE
COMPANIES AND
WRITTEN
RESOLUTIONS

In earlier chapters reference has been made to written resolutions and elective resolutions, both of which were introduced by the Companies Act 1989. We will now look at what is meant by them. Written resolutions have been around for many years by voluntary arrangements under the articles of association. What we have now is a statutory right for private companies. The 'elective regime', which is totally new, allows private companies to dispense with various administrative and procedural requirements.

12.1 UNANIMOUS WRITTEN RESOLUTIONS

As indicated above, a company's articles commonly provide for resolutions of members to be passed in writing rather than at a general meeting, for example, regulation 53 of Table A.

The Companies Act 1989 provides an express statutory basis for written resolutions of private companies. In so doing, it places various limitations and conditions on the use of the written resolution procedure. It should be noted that the provisions in the Act override anything to the contrary in the memorandum or articles.

Anything which a private company may do:

1. by resolution in general meeting; or
2. by resolution of a class meeting;

may be done instead by a written resolution signed by all the members who would be entitled to attend and vote at such a meeting at the date the resolution is signed by or on behalf of the last member to sign. The signatures need not be on a single document provided each is on a document which accurately states the terms of the resolution (section 381A(1) & (2)).

Written resolutions will not be effective for the purpose of removing a director or an auditor before the end of his/her term of office (schedule 15A, paragraph 1).

The written resolution procedure may be used to pass resolutions which would otherwise be required to be passed as special, extraordinary or elective resolutions (see paragraph 12.2 below). Any such resolution must be filed with the Registrar within 15 days of it being signed by or on behalf of the last member to sign (subject to the following procedure involving the auditors having been completed) (section 381A(6)).

A copy of any written resolution proposed to be passed must be sent to the company's auditors. If the resolution concerns the auditors as auditors, they may notify the company within seven days that in their opinion a meeting should be called to consider it. The resolution will then not have effect unless a meeting is held. The auditors should be encouraged to respond within the seven days even if they do not require a meeting to be held or if the matter does not concern them as auditors, otherwise the duly signed written resolution does not take effect until the conclusion of the seven day notification period (section 381B(1)).

Duly signed written resolutions must be recorded in a minute book in the same way as minutes of a general meeting of the company (section 382A(1)).

The Act (schedule 15A, paragraphs 3–8) provides for special procedural requirements to apply in the case of written resolutions concerning the following matters:

1. disapplication of pre-emption rights on the issue of shares for cash;
2. financial assistance for the purchase of a company's own shares or those of its holding company (see Chapter 15);
3. authority for an off-market purchase or contingent purchase contract of a company's own shares (see paragraph 14.1);

4. approval for payments out of capital on a redemption or purchase of a company's own shares (see paragraph 14.2(C));
5. approval of a director's contract of employment for more than five years; and
6. approval of funding of a director's expenditure in performing his/her duties.

In each case, certain matters must be disclosed to members before, or at the same time as, the resolution is sent to them for signature. In the case of 3 and 4, the signatures of the members whose shares are being bought are not required.

12.2 ELECTIVE REGIME

To relieve some of the administrative burdens on many private companies, particularly when the directors and shareholders are the same, the Act has given such companies the power to make certain elections. There are five in total, the first three being of most value as they affect the annual requirements of companies.

12.3 LAYING OF ACCOUNTS AND REPORTS

A private company may elect to dispense with the laying of accounts and reports before the members in general meeting. An election has effect in relation to the accounts and reports in respect of the financial year in which it is made and subsequent financial years. It is therefore not possible to elect to dispense with the laying of accounts and reports in respect of a financial year which has already ended (section 252).

If an election is made, the accounts and reports would still have to be sent to members. They must be sent not less than 28 days before the end of the ten month period allowed for private companies to lay and deliver accounts and reports. With the accounts there is a requirement for a notice informing members of their right to require the accounts to be laid before a general meeting. Such a notice could conveniently be included in the directors' report (section 253(1)).

Any one member or the auditor may, within 28 days of the date on which the accounts are sent out, give written notice to the company at its registered office requiring the accounts to be laid before a general meeting. The directors are then required to convene a meeting, within 21 days from the date the notice is received, for a date not more than 28 days after the date the meeting is convened (section 253(2), (3) & (6)).

12.4 ANNUAL GENERAL MEETINGS (AGMs)

If a company elects not to lay accounts before the members in general meeting it follows that a private company may elect to dispense with the holding of AGMs. An election has effect for the year in which it is made and subsequent years (section 366A(1) & (2)).

If an election is made, any member may require an annual general meeting to be held in any calendar year, by notifying the company accordingly at least three months before the end of that year. A company which elects to dispense with AGMs is still required to lay accounts and reports before its members in general meeting unless it has also elected to dispense with this (see paragraph 12.3) (section 366A(3)).

12.5 ANNUAL APPOINTMENT OF AUDITORS

Auditors are normally re-elected at AGMs. With the possibility of electing to dispense with AGMs a provision is also given for a private company to elect to dispense with the annual appointment of auditors (section 386).

12.6 DURATION OF DIRECTORS' AUTHORITY TO ALLOT SHARES

A private company may elect that an authority for directors to allot shares, up to a specified maximum amount, may be given for an indefinite period or for a fixed period of any duration (as opposed to a maximum period of five years) (section 80A).

12.7 SHORT NOTICE OF MEETINGS/RESOLUTIONS

A private company may elect to reduce the 95% majority (by nominal value of voting shares) required for the following purposes to a minimum of 90%:

1. Authorizing the holding of a meeting (other than the AGM) at

short notice. Unanimous consent is still required to hold the AGM at short notice (but the company may elect to dispense with the holding of AGMs; see paragraph 12.4 above) (section 369(4)).

2. Agreeing to the passing of a special resolution at a meeting of which less than 21 days' notice has been given (section 378(3)).

12.8 ELECTIVE RESOLUTIONS

The mechanism for taking advantage of the various relaxations outlined above (paragraphs 12.3–12.7) is the passing of an 'elective resolution' (section 379A(1) & (2)). An elective resolution is not effective unless:

1. it is passed unanimously (whether at a meeting or in writing) by all members entitled to vote; and
2. 21 days' notice is given of the meeting (where applicable).

An elective resolution may be revoked by passing an ordinary resolution to that effect. It automatically ceases to have effect if the company is re-registered as a public company (section 379A(3) & (4)).

An elective resolution may be passed for any of the purposes outlined above (paragraphs 12.3–12.7), notwithstanding any contrary provision in the company's articles. For example, a company may pass an elective resolution to dispense with the holding of AGMs even if the articles require one to be held (section 379A(5)).

Elective resolutions and resolutions revoking them have to be filed with the Registrar within 15 days (in the same way as special resolutions and extraordinary resolutions).

13

RE-REGISTRATION AS
A PUBLIC COMPANY

Re-registration as a public company enables a company to offer its shares and/or debentures to the public and to obtain a listing on the Stock Exchange.

13.1 ADVANTAGES AND DISADVANTAGES OF RE-REGISTRATION

The disadvantages of re-registration may be summarized as follows:

1. A public company has to meet the 'authorized minimum' subscribed capital (sections 45(2)(a) & 118(1)).
2. It is necessary for the allotted shares to be paid up to at least one quarter of their nominal amount, plus the whole of any premium (section 45(2)(b)).
3. The memorandum must contain a clause stating that the company is a public company (section 1(3)(a)).
4. A public company may only commence business on the issue of a trade certificate by the Registrar (section 117)).
5. A public company cannot have one director (section 282(1)).
6. The reappointment of directors in general meeting cannot be effected by a single resolution. Each director must be re-appointed by a separate resolution (section 292(1)).
7. The provisions relating to the retirement of directors on reaching the age limit apply to such companies (section 293(3)).
8. At a general meeting a proxy may not address the meeting (section 372(1)).
9. The provisions regulating insider dealing apply only to Stock Exchange dealings and therefore do not apply to private

companies (The Companies Securities (Insider Dealing) Act 1985).

10. Pre-emption rights cannot be excluded by the memorandum or the articles (sections 89 & 91).

11. Many of the provisions of the 1985 Act regulating directors' dealings with their companies apply only to public companies and to private companies which form part of a group including a public company (e.g. the restrictions in section 330(3) and (4) which apply only to relevant companies as defined in section 331(6)).

12. An expert's valuation report is required if a public company wishes to acquire certain non-cash assets during its first two years from a subscriber or member (section 104).

13. It would be necessary to call an extraordinary general meeting in the event of the company losing half or more of its called-up share capital to consider what measures should be taken (section 142).

14. Only a private company limited by guarantee can be exempt from ending its name in the word 'limited' (section 30).

15. A public company may not give financial assistance for the purchase of its own shares (section 155 relaxes the prohibition on such assistance for private companies).

16. A public company may not redeem or purchase its own shares out of capital (section 171 allows private companies to do so).

17. A public company is not eligible to file abbreviated (or 'modified') accounts as a small or medium-sized company. The parent company of a group containing a public company is not eligible for the exemption for the parents of small and medium-sized groups from the obligation to prepare group accounts. Such a parent company is also not eligible to file abbreviated accounts (sections 246 & 248).

18. A public company has less time to lay its financial statements before members and deliver them to the Registrar (seven months from the end of its accounting reference period as against ten months for a private company) (section 244). In addition, a public company cannot elect to dispense with the requirement to lay financial statements before the members in general meeting (under section 252).

19. There are greater restrictions upon what a public company may distribute by way of dividend (section 264).

20. A public company cannot elect to:
    (a) dispense with the holding of Annual General Meetings (under section 366A);

(b) dispense with the annual appointment of auditors (under section 386);

(c) authorize the directors to allot shares, up to a specified maximum amount, indefinitely or for a fixed period in excess of five years (under section 80A); or

(d) reduce the majority required to authorize short notice of a meeting (under section 369(4)).

13.2 RE-REGISTRATION PROCEDURE

The procedure to re-register a private company as a public company is as follows:

1. A special resolution is passed that the company be re-registered as a public company and altering the memorandum of the company to state that the company is to be a public company and making any other amendments necessary to make the memorandum (and articles) conform with the requirements for the memorandum of a public company (e.g. the requirement for the name of the company to end with the appropriate suffix — public limited company or plc, or their Welsh equivalents) (section 43(2)).

2. An application for re-registration is submitted to the Registrar on form 43(3) signed by a director or the secretary, together with:

   (a) A printed copy of the memorandum and articles as altered by the special resolution.

   (b) A copy of a statement by the auditors that in their opinion the relevant balance sheet (i.e. a balance sheet prepared as at a date not more than seven months before the application) shows that at the balance sheet date the amount of the company's net assets was not less than the aggregate of its called-up share capital and undistributable reserves.

   (c) A copy of the relevant balance sheet, together with a copy of an unqualified auditors' report thereon.

   (d) A statutory declaration on form 43(3)(e), by a director or the secretary of the company, that:

      (i) The required special resolution was duly passed.

      (ii) There has been no change, between the date of the relevant balance sheet and the application for re-registration, in the company's financial position that has resulted in the amount of the company's net assets becoming less than the aggregate of its called-up share capital and undistributable reserves.

3. It should be noted that:
   (a) Only private companies limited by shares may re-register (section 43(1)).
   (b) A minimum issued share capital of £50 000 is required, of which 25% must be paid-up together with the whole of any premium (sections 45(2) & 118).
   (c) A re-registration fee of £50 is payable.
   (d) Re-registration is not effective until the Registrar issues his/her certificate of re-registration (section 47).
   (e) A change of name can be effected simultaneously if included in the same special resolution.

14

PURCHASE OF A COMPANY'S OWN SHARE

14.1 GENERAL

The Companies Act 1985 provides for a company to purchase its own shares whether or not they were issued originally as redeemable shares. A public company may purchase its own shares on the market and off the market. As this guide is principally concerned with private companies, we will not therefore deal with market purchases (section 162(1)).

Before any off-market purchase can be made, the articles must be examined to see whether they provide for the repurchase of shares. Table A in The Companies (Tables A to F) Regulations 1985 provides for the repurchase of shares. Companies formed prior to the 1981 Act and having articles based on the Table A previously in force will not have the repurchase provision, unless their articles have subsequently been amended by special resolution.

A special resolution must be passed for the purpose of approving a proposed contract to purchase the shares (either at an EGM or by means of a written resolution). It must state the terms on which those shares are to be purchased. A copy of the proposed contract or, if not in writing, a memorandum of its terms, must be available at the registered office of the company at least 14 days prior to the holding of an Extraordinary General Meeting (section 164). Given the need for a copy of the proposed contract to be made available for 14 days prior to a meeting, it is not possible to shorten the notice period to less than the period of 14 days, excluding the date of the meeting.

If the approval is to be given by means of a written resolution, the signature of a member holding shares to which the resolution relates is not required. In addition, a copy of the proposed contract must be supplied to each relevant member at or before the time the resolution is supplied for signature (schedule 15A, paragraph 5).

Following the passing of the special resolution or adoption of the written resolution (as the case may be), the directors would be authorized to enter into the contract, repurchase shares and pay over the consideration to the transferor. A return (form 169) has to be made to the Registrar of Companies within 28 days after the repurchase of the shares. Stamp duty at a rate of 50p per £100 of consideration or part thereof is payable on the return (section 169).

14.2 PURCHASE OUT OF CAPITAL

A private company may purchase its own shares out of capital if authorized to do so by its articles. The amount which may be paid out of capital ('the permissible capital payment') is equal to the price of redemption or purchase less any available profits and the proceeds of any new issue of shares made for the purpose (section 171(1).(3)).

The following apply to a payment out of capital (sections 173–175):

1. The directors must make a statutory declaration stating:
    (a) the amount of the permissible capital payment;
    (b) that there will be no grounds on which the company could be found to be unable to pay its debts immediately following the payment; and
    (c) that the company will be able to carry on business as a going concern throughout the following year.
2. The auditors must make a report to the directors in connection with the statutory declaration.
3. A special resolution approving the payment out of capital must be passed on, or within seven days of, the date of the directors' statutory declaration. This can be done either at an EGM convened for the purpose or by means of a written resolution (see paragraph 12.1(d)).
4. Within seven days of the date of the resolution, a notice of the proposed capital payment must be placed in the *London Gazette*. In addition, either a notice must be placed in a national newspaper or written notice given to each creditor.
5. The directors' statutory declaration, with the auditors' report

annexed thereto, must be filed with the Registrar not later than the date the notice required by 4 above is first published.

6. The payment out of capital cannot be made earlier than five weeks nor later than seven weeks after the date of the resolution.

Where the approval of the payment out of capital is to be given by written resolution, a member holding shares to which the resolution relates is not to be regarded as a member who would be entitled to attend and vote at a meeting (his/her signature is therefore not required). In addition, the directors' statutory declaration and the auditors' report thereon must be supplied to each relevant member at or before the time the resolution is supplied to him/her for signature (schedule 15A, paragraph 6).

15

FINANCIAL ASSISTANCE FOR THE PURCHASE OF OWN SHARES

15.1 GENERAL

Generally it is not lawful for a company or any of its subsidiaries to give direct or indirect financial assistance for the purpose of an acquisition of its shares, actual or proposed. 'Financial assistance' is widely defined and is not simply the provision of finance to a proposed shareholder or the guaranteeing of any loan or finance provided by a third party to that shareholder (sections 151 & 152).

15.2 EXCEPTIONS TO THE GENERAL RULE

The principle that financial assistance is generally prohibited is subject to certain exceptions. For example, assistance may be provided if the company's principal purpose in giving assistance is an incidental part of some larger purpose of the company and it is given in good faith in the interests of the company. Other cases where financial assistance is permitted include the provision of assistance for the purposes of an employees' share scheme (defined in section 743). Since 1 April 1990, any form of financial assistance, provided it is given in good faith in the interests of the company, may be provided for this purpose (for example, a guarantee to a bank which makes a loan to a scheme or the repayment of capital or interest charged on such a loan) (section 153).

15.3 GENERAL EXCEPTION FOR PRIVATE COMPANIES

For private companies there is a general relaxation of the prohibition on the giving of assistance, provided the company has net assets which would not thereby be reduced or, to the extent that they are reduced, the excess is financed from distributable profits (sections 155–158). The following procedures apply:

1. The directors of the company and of any holding company involved must make a statutory declaration in the prescribed form (form 155(6)) stating:
   (a) that the company proposes to give financial assistance in connection with the acquisition of its own shares;
   (b) the purpose for giving the assistance;
   (c) details of the business of the company of which they are directors (if the company is not a bank or an insurance company, one simply states 'something other than the above');
   (d) the number and class of the shares acquired or to be acquired; and
   (e) the person to whom assistance is to be given and the form that the assistance will take.

2. The statutory declaration must also state the directors' opinion that there will be no grounds on which the company could be found to be unable to pay its debts immediately after the provision of the assistance and either:
   (a) that the company will be able to pay its debts as they fall due during the following year; or
   (b) if the winding up of the company is intended to commence within the following year, that the company will be able to pay its debts in full within 12 months of the commencement of the winding up.

3. The auditors must make a report to the directors in connection with the statutory declaration.

4. A special resolution approving the giving of the assistance must be passed on, or within seven days of, the date of the directors' statutory declaration. This can be done either at an EGM convened for the purpose or by means of a written resolution (see below and paragraph 12.1). Where the financial assistance is to be given by a subsidiary to acquire shares in its holding company, a special resolution approving it must also be passed by the members of that holding company. Where a wholly-owned subsidiary is providing the assistance, that wholly-owned subsidi-

ary need not approve the giving of the assistance (just the holding company).

5. The directors' statutory declaration, with the auditors' report annexed thereto, and the special resolution must be filed with the Registrar within 15 days.

6. Unless the special resolution was passed unanimously, the assistance cannot be given until four weeks after the date the resolution was passed. It must not be given later than eight weeks after the date of the directors' statutory declaration. During the four week period, application may be made to the court by holders of not less than 10% in aggregate in nominal value of the company's issued share capital for the resolution to be cancelled. An advantage of using the written resolution procedure is that the resolution must be passed unanimously and the four week waiting period is therefore avoided.

Where the approval of the financial assistance is to be given by written resolution, the directors' statutory declaration and the auditors' report thereon must be supplied to each relevant member at or before the time the resolution is supplied to him/her for signature (schedule 15A, paragraph 4).

16

DORMANT
COMPANIES

16.1 DEFINITION

A company is 'dormant' during a period in which no significant accounting transaction occurs (i.e. no transaction which is required to be entered in the company's accounting records). Transactions arising from the taking of shares in the company by a subscriber to the memorandum are to be disregarded (section 250(3)).

16.2 EXEMPTION FROM OBLIGATION TO APPOINT AUDITORS

A company may, by special resolution, make itself exempt from the obligation to appoint auditors in the following cases:

1. If it has been dormant from the time of its formation by a special resolution passed before the first general meeting of the company at which financial statements are laid.
2. If it has been dormant since the end of the previous financial year and:
   (a) is entitled to the exemptions available to small companies; and
   (b) is not required to prepare group accounts;
   by a special resolution passed at a general meeting of the company at which the financial statements for that year are laid (section 250(1)).

16.3 COMPANIES ALWAYS REQUIRING AUDITS

The following companies may not pass a resolution to exempt themselves from the requirement to appoint auditors:

1. a public company;
2. a banking or insurance company;
3. a company which is an authorized person under the Financial Services Act 1986.

16.4 RULES AFFECTING THE ACCOUNTS

Where a company is, at the end of a financial year, exempt from appointing auditors under paragraph 16.2:

1. The financial statements need not include an auditors' report.
2. The company shall be treated in respect of its individual accounts as entitled to the exemptions available to small companies, notwithstanding that it is a member of an ineligible group (a group of companies which includes a company referred to in 16.3 above).

A dormant company's financial statements would contain the following:

1. an abbreviated balance sheet;
2. no profit and loss accounts (except for the first year in which it becomes dormant since there is a requirement to disclose previous year's figures when there are no current year figures);
3. abbreviated notes to the accounts;
4. no directors' report.

16.5 DORMANT COMPANY ACCOUNTS

Although dormant companies may exempt themselves from appointing auditors, they are still required to prepare and file accounts. A specimen set of dormant company accounts is included in the Appendix D, P31.

17

THE END OF THE ROAD

17.1 ALTERNATIVE METHODS OF DISPOSAL

There comes a time in the case of some companies when their useful life comes to an end. The requirement to prepare annual accounts is a rather onerous obligation if the company is serving no useful purpose. The members or directors may therefore wish to dispose of the company. There are three alternative methods of disposal:

1. the formal liquidation of the company;
2. the directors requesting the Registrar to strike the company off; or
3. the Registrar him/herself deciding to strike the company off.

17.2 FORMAL LIQUIDATION

A formal liquidation is quite expensive since it involves appointing liquidators and posting notice by way of advertisement in the *London Gazette*.

17.3 STRIKING OFF

Striking off by directors

The second method involves the directors, having first obtained the consent of the shareholders, asking the Registrar to exercise his/her powers under section 652. The request must be accompanied by an assurance that the company is dormant and has not traded since a stated date (normally the last year-end) and that it has no assets or liabilities. At the same time Form 288, stating that all officers of the company resigned on the date given in the form, should be filed. The Registrar will then follow the procedures outlined in the following paragraph.

Striking off by Registrar

The third method involves no effort whatsoever on the part of the company and its officers. Under section 652, the Registrar is entitled to initiate the procedure to strike off a company if he/she believes that it is not carrying on business or is not in operation. Indicators will be failure to file accounts and annual returns as required. The Registrar must write to the company to see if it is still operational. If he gets no reply, he publishes a notice in the *London Gazette*. Three months later, if there is no response, he can strike off the company and publish another notice to that effect. The company is then automatically dissolved.

The second and third methods leave the directors of the company at some degree of risk. Under section 652(6), the liability of the directors, managing officer and members of the company continues and may be enforced as if the company had not been dissolved. This can result in serious consequences and should not be taken lightly. It should also be noted that the Inland Revenue sometimes object to the striking off of individual companies.

17.4 TAX IMPLICATIONS OF DISPOSAL

Each method involves the disposal of shares for the purposes of capital gains tax. If there are no assets or liabilities available, there are no consequences to consider. If there are assets or liabilities, it is important to ensure that all tax computations have been agreed with the Inland Revenue and an up-to-date assessment made of any liability on investment income or remuneration paid from the company. It is probable, however, that there will be no major transactions or income.

Having obtained an estimate of all outstanding tax liabilities and made a reserve for tax due from the company in respect of corporation tax, stamp duties, etc. the balance of assets are available for distribution. The distribution of the assets will give rise to two possible tax liabilities:

1. The distribution to the shareholders may give rise to capital gains tax in the hands of the individual shareholders. In a formal liquidation, the date of disposal will be the separate dates on which consideration is received for each part disposal of assets which constitutes a liquidation. Some modifying provisions are granted by the Revenue should the liquidation be completed within one year.
2. The disposal of the assets into cash or distribution of the assets to the shareholders in specie is a deemed disposal and may give rise to capital gains tax. The appropriate reserve must be made. Under the second and third methods, the date of disposal will be the date of striking off. Any property held by the company immediately before dissolution becomes *bona vacantia* and rests in the Crown. All right to and ownership of valuable assets is lost. It could be argued that no consideration is paid for the shares.

The following points should also be noted:

1. The individual circumstances of the company and of its shareholders must be examined very carefully.
2. The Inland Revenue can and do object to the striking off of individual companies.

APPENDIX A

Statutory registers and books

	Companies Act, 1985
Register of members	sections 352 and 353
Register of charges	section 407
Register of directors and secretaries	sections 288, 289 and 230
Register of directors' interests in shares and debentures	sections 325, 326 and schedule 13, part 12
Register of interests in voting shares (if a plc)	section 211
Minute books of the proceedings of meetings of the company and its directors	section 382
Accounting records	sections 221, 222 and 223

A register of debenture holders is not required by the Act but if one is kept it is governed by sections 190 and 191.

In addition to the above, a company would normally maintain registers of allotments and transfers with its register of members but these two registers are not required by the Act.

APPENDIX B

Events requiring notification to or filing with the Registrar of Companies in respect of United Kingdom companies

Directors

Appointment, resignation, removal or death; any change of address, name or other particulars (notification required within 14 days of change).

Secretary

Appointment, resignation, removal or death; any change of address or name (notification required within 14 days of change).

Registered office

Any change (notification required within 14 days of change).

Location of register of members and/or debentures

If the register of members and/or debentures is kept or is to be kept at a place other than at the company's registered office notification is required of that location or of any change.

Accounting reference date

Any change (there are time restraints as to how and when an accounting reference date can be changed).

Accounts

These must be filed within seven months for plcs and ten months for private companies of the conclusion of the accounting reference period to which they relate.

Extension of filing period for accounts

To take advantage of the three months' extension for companies having interests overseas, annual notification is required within the normal filing period, i.e. seven months for plcs and ten months for private companies.

Annual returns

An annual return made up to a date not later than the company's 'return date' and filed within the succeeding four weeks.

Share capital

Any change in the authorized or issued capital (notification required within 15 days and 30 days respectively). Any transfer of shares recorded in the statutory books would be notified to the Registrar on the next annual return following the event.

Mortgages and charges

Particulars of any mortgages or charges (notification required within 21 days of creation) and the satisfaction or part satisfaction of any mortgage or charge.

Changes to the memorandum and articles of association

Any amendment must be notified within 15 days of the passing of the relevant resolution together with a copy of the memorandum and/or articles as amended. Where the objects clause of the memorandum is amended, the amended copy need not be filed until 36 days after the passing of the resolution.

Change of auditors, etc.

The resignation or removal of an auditor must be notified within 14 days of the receipt or effective date of the resignation or of the date of the passing of the resolution removing the auditor. The appointment of an auditor does not require notification. Dormant companies which take advantage of section 252, Companies Act 1985 must file the special resolution not to appoint or reappoint auditors within 15 days of the passing of the resolution.

APPENDIX C

Company and business names

Where a proposed company or business name incorporates any of the words or expressions in the left-hand column below, or may give the impression of some connection with the government or any local authority, prior approval must be obtained from the Secretary of State and (where applicable) the relevant body referred to in the second column, before that name can be registered and/or used.

Word or expression	Relevant body
Abortion	Department of Health
Apothecary	Worshipful Company of Apothecaries of London or Pharmaceutical Society of Great Britain
Association	
Assurance	
Assurer	
Authority	
Benevolent	
Board	
Breed	
Breeder	Ministry of Agriculture, Fisheries and Food
Breeding	
British	
Building Society	
Chamber of Commerce	
Chamber of Industry	

Word or expression	Relevant body
Chamber of Trade	
Charitable	
Charity	Charity Commission
Charter	
Chartered	
Chemist	
Chemistry	
Contact Lens	General Optical Council
Co-operative	
Council	
Dental	General Dental Council
Dentistry	
District Nurse	English National Board for Nursing Midwifery and Health Visiting
Duke	Home Office
England	
English	
European	
Federation	
Friendly Society	
Foundation	
Fund	
Giro	
Great Britain	
Group	
Health Centre	Department of Health
Health Service	
Health Visitor	[see District Nurse]
Her Majesty	Home Office
His Majesty	
Holding	
Industrial and Provident Society	
Institute	
Institution	
Insurance	
Insurer	
International	
Ireland	
Irish	
King	Home Office

Word or expression	Relevant body
Midwife	[see District Nurse]
Midwifery	
National	
Nurse	[see District Nurse]
Nursing	
Nursing Home	Department of Health
Patent	
Patentee	
Police	Home Office
Polytechnic	Department of Education and Science
Post Office	
Pregnancy Termination	Department of Health
Prince	
Princess	
	Home Office
Queen	
Reassurance	
Reassurer	
Register	
Registered	
Reinsurance	
Reinsurer	
Royal	
Royale	Home Office
Royalty	
Scotland	
Scottish	
Sheffield	
Society	
Special School	Department of Education and Science
Stock Exchange	
Trade Union	
Trust	
United Kingdom	
University	Department of Education and Science
Wales	
Welsh	
Windsor	Home Office

Reference should also be made to sections 28(2) and 29, Companies Act 1985 and sections 2 and 3, Business Names Act 1985. The above words and expression were taken from The Company and Business Names Regulations 1981 (SI 1981 No. 1685) as amended by The Company and Business Names (Amendment) Regulations 1982 (SI 1982 No. 1653) to which reference should also be made.

Other words which may require consent or confirmation from a relevant body before use include the following (the list is not exhaustive):

Word or expression	Relevant Act	Relevant body
Anzac	Anzac	Advice from Companies House
Architect Architectural	Architects' Registration Act 1938	Architects' Registration Council of the United Kingdom
Bank Banker Banking Deposit	Banking Act 1979	Bank of England
Credit Union	Credit Union Act 1979	Registry of Friendly Societies
Dentist Dental Surgeon Dental Practitioner	Dentist Act 1984	General Dental Council
Drug Druggist Pharmaceutical Pharmaceutist Pharmacist Pharmacy	Medicines Act 1968	The Pharmaceutical Society of Great Britain
Insurance Broker Assurance Broker Reinsurance Broker Reassurance Broker	Insurance Broker (Registration) Act	Advice from Companies House
Chiropodist Dietician Medical Laboratory Technician Occupational Therapist Optometrist Physiotherapist Radiotherapist Remedial Gymnast	Professions Supplementary to Medicines Act 1960 (if preceded by 'Registered', 'State Registered' or 'State')	Department of Health
Optician Ophthalmic Optician Dispensing Optician Enrolled Optician Registered Optician Optometrist	Opticians Act 1958 and Health and Social Security Act 1984	General Optical Council
Red Cross	Geneva Convention Act 1957	Advice from Companies House
Veterinary Surgeon	Veterinary Surgeons Act 1966	Royal College of Veterinary Surgeons

APPENDIX D

Standard resolutions and minutes

Many of the precedents that follow have been referred to in the text of the handbook — the rest are additional ones which you should find helpful.

The precedents have in the main been set out in the form of either full minutes of a directors' meeting together with a notice of an Extraordinary or Annual General Meeting and the minutes of the Extraordinary or Annual General Meeting or (in place of an Extraordinary General Meeting) written resolution. This is to enable you to appreciate the two differing styles of passing resolutions. Even when the written resolution method is followed a minute of a directors' meeting referring to the need to put a specific matter to the members (shareholders) should be prepared. Please remember that the removal of a director or the auditor cannot be effected by a written resolution.

P1. MEMBERS' RESOLUTION TO CHANGE COMPANY NAME/OBJECTS/SHARE CAPITAL

[NAME IN FULL] LIMITED

RESOLUTIONS signed by all the Shareholders of the Company for the time being pursuant to section 381A, Companies Act 1985.

RESOLUTIONS

1. **That** the name of the Company be changed to:

   [NAME IN FULL] LIMITED

2. **That** the provisions of the Memorandum of Association of the Company be altered by deleting sub-clauses (A) and (B) of clause 3 thereof and substituting therefor the following sub-clauses:

   [insert new objects clauses]

3. **That** the authorized Share Capital of the Company be increased to £[value] by the creation of [number] additional shares of £[value] each which shall be at the disposal of the directors who may allot or otherwise dispose of them or grant options over them to such persons (including any director) at such times and generally on such terms and conditions (subject to section 100, Companies Act 1985) as they think proper **and that** the authority conferred on the directors by this Resolution shall expire on the 5th anniversary of the passing of this Resolution but may be renewed, varied or extended by the Company in General Meeting from time to time.

Dated: [date]

....
[name]

....
[name]

....
[name]

....
[name]

No. [number]

The Companies Act 1985
Company Limited by Shares

WRITTEN RESOLUTION

of

[NAME IN FULL] LIMITED

(Passed [date])

By a written resolution signed, pursuant to section 381A, Companies Act 1985, by or on behalf of all the members of the Company entitled to attend and vote at general meetings, the following resolution was duly agreed on [date].

RESOLUTION

That the name of the Company be changed to:

[NAME IN FULL] LIMITED

....
DIRECTOR

P2. ALTERATION OF ARTICLES

SPECIAL RESOLUTION (Company in general meeting) or Written Resolution to alter articles of association

A. (To amend text)
    That the articles of association of the company be altered as follows:

    (a) by deleting in article [number] the words
    ('words to be deleted'];

    (b) by substituting for the existing article [number] the
    following article:
    ['article to be inserted']; and

    (c) by deleting in article [number] the words
    ['words to be deleted'] and substituting therefor the words
    ['words to be inserted']

B. (To adopt new articles)

    That the regulations contained in the [printed] document [marked 'B'] submitted to this meeting and, for the purpose of identification, signed by the chairman hereof be approved and adopted as the articles of association of the company in substitution for and to the exclusion of all the existing articles thereof.

P3. FIRST DIRECTORS' MEETING

[NAME IN FULL] LIMITED

MINUTES OF THE FIRST MEETING OF THE DIRECTORS

HELD AT [address]

ON [date] at [time]

PRESENT: [name] (In the Chair)
                [name]
                [name]
                [name]

1. Incorporation of company

It was reported that the Company had been incorporated on [date] and the Certificate of Incorporation numbered [number] together with a print of the Memorandum and Articles of Association in the form in which they were registered with the Registrar of Companies were produced to the Meeting.

2.A First directors

The meeting took formal note that [name] and [name] were appointed the first directors of the Company pursuant to section 13(5), Companies Act 1985.

2.B Appointment of addition directors

It was resolved that [name] and [name] be and are each hereby appointed a Director of the Company. They thereupon took their place at the Meeting as Directors.

2.C Disclosure of interest

In accordance with section 317 of the Companies Act 1985 [name] and [name] each formally disclosed to the Meeting pursuant to Regulations 85 and 86 of Table A in the Companies (Tables A to F) Regulations 1985 his/her interest as a Shareholder and/or Director as follows: [details of disclosures of interest].

2.D Resignation of directors

There were produced to the Meeting letters addressed to the Company from [name] and from [name] both dated [date] in which they each tendered their resignation as a Director of the Company and in which they each confirmed that they had no outstanding claims against the Company in respect of any matter whatsoever. **It was resolved** ([name] and [name] abstaining from voting on the Resolution) that each resignation be and is hereby accepted. [name] and [name] thereupon ceased to take any further proceedings in the Meeting as Directors.

3.A First secretary

The Meeting took formal note that [name] had been appointed Secretary of the Company pursuant to section 13(5), Companies Act 1985.

3.B Resignation of secretary

There was produced to the Meeting a letter from [name] to the Company dated [date] containing his resignation as Secretary of the Company and **it was resolved** that his resignation as Secretary be and is hereby accepted.

3.C Appointment of secretary

It was resolved that [name] be and is hereby appointed Secretary of the Company.

4.A Registered office

The Meeting took formal note that the Company's registered office pursuant to section 10(6), Companies Act 1985 is at: [address].

4.B Change of registered office

It was resolved that the Company's registered office be and is hereby changed to: [address].

5. Election of chairman

It was resolved ([name] abstaining from voting on the Resolution) that [name] be and is hereby elected Chairman of the Company.

6. Adoption of seal

The Secretary produced to the Meeting a Seal bearing the Company's name, an impression of which Seal appears in the margin against this resolution, and **it was resolved** that such Seal be and is hereby adopted as the Common Seal of the Company.

```
┌─────────────────────┐
│                     │
│   [impression of    │
│        seal]        │
│                     │
└─────────────────────┘
```

7. Appointment of bankers

It was resolved that [name] of [address] be and is hereby appointed Bankers to the Company in the terms of their Form of Appointment annexed to these Minutes and signed by the Chairman for the purposes of identification **and that** such Form of Appointment be and is hereby deemed to be incorporated in these Minutes except insofar as it has been altered and amended.

8. Appointment of auditors

It was resolved that Messrs [name], of [address] be and are hereby appointed Auditors of the Company pursuant to section 384(2), Companies Act 1985.

9. Subscribers' shares

It was resolved that each of the subscribers to the Memorandum of Association be entered in the Registrar of Members as the holder of the Share for which he had agreed to subscribe.

10. Transfer of subscribers' shares

There were produced to the Meeting transfers of each of the subscribers' shares as follows:

TRANSFEROR	NUMBER OF SHARES	TRANSFEREE
[name]	One	[name]
[name]	One	[name]

It was resolved that the transfers be approved and registered and that the relative Share Certificates be [sealed and] issued to the Transferees.

11. Allotment of shares

There were presented to the Meeting applications for shares in the capital of the

Company together with cheques covering the subscription monies and **it was resolved** that shares of £[value] each of the Company be allotted fully paid to the Applicants whose names are set out in the first column below and so that each Applicant shall receive an allotment of the number of shares specified in the second column below opposite his or her name and that all such shares do rank *pari passu* in all respects.

NAME	NUMBER OF SHARES
[name]	[number]
[name]	[number]
[name]	[number]
[name]	[number]

It was further resolved that Certificates in respect of the shares hereby allotted be [sealed and] issued to the respective allottees.

12. Accounting reference date

It was resolved that the accounting reference date of the Company for the purposes of section 224(2), Companies Act 1985 be [date (without year) being the ARD] in each year and that the first set of accounts be prepared for the period from Incorporation of the Company to [date being end of first ARP].

13. Filing of documents

The Secretary produced to the Meeting the following returns for filing at the Companies Registry:
 (i) Form No. 288 in respect of the changes of Directors and Secretary.
 (ii) Form No. 287 in respect of the change in registered office.
 (iii) Form No. 88(2) in respect of the allotment of shares.
 (iv) Form No. 224 in respect of the accounting reference date.
It was resolved that each form be and is hereby approved **and that** the Secretary be and is hereby authorized and directed to sign each of them on behalf of the Company and arrange for them to be filed at the Companies Registry.

....
[name]
CHAIRMAN

P4. LETTERS OF RESIGNATION

Director

[RESIDENTIAL HOME ADDRESS]

[DATE]

The Directors
[NAME IN FULL] LIMITED

Dear Sirs

I hereby resign as a Director of [NAME IN FULL] LIMITED with immediate effect and confirm I have no outstanding claim against the Company in respect of any matter whatsoever.

Yours faithfully

....
[name]

Secretary

[RESIDENTIAL HOME ADDRESS]

[DATE]

The Directors
[NAME IN FULL] LIMITED

Dear Sirs

I hereby resign as Secretary of [NAME IN FULL] LIMITED with immediate effect.

Yours faithfully

....
[name]

P5. FORM OF APPLICATION FOR SHARES (suitable for a private company)

The Directors   [date]
[Name in full] Limited

I enclose a cheque for £[amount], being payment in full for [number] shares of £[value] each in [name] Limited, and I hereby apply for and request you to allot such shares to me.

I agree to take the said shares subject to the memorandum and articles of association of the company and I authorize you to enter my name in the register of members as the holder of the said shares.

Dated: [date]

....
[name]
[address]

P6. BONUS ISSUE

[NAME IN FULL] LIMITED

MINUTES OF A MEETING OF THE DIRECTORS

HELD AT [address]

ON [date]

PRESENT: [name] (In the Chair)
                       [name]
                       [name]
                       [name]

1. Extraordinary general meeting

It was resolved that an Extraordinary General Meeting be convened and held forthwith for the purpose of increasing the authorized Share Capital to £[value] and capitalizing £[value] out of reserves, in accordance with the Notice presented to the Meeting.

(The Meeting was then adjourned to allow the Extraordinary General Meeting to take place).

On reconvening, the Chairman reported that both the Resolutions proposed at the Extraordinary General Meeting had been passed unanimously.

2. Allotment of shares

Having regard to the Resolution passed at the Extraordinary General Meeting to capitalize the sum of £[value] out of reserves, **It was resolved** that shares of £1 each of the Company be allotted to the persons whose names are set out in the first column below and so that each person shall receive the number of shares specified in the second column below opposite his name.

Name	No. of shares
[name]	[number]
[name]	[number]
[name]	[number]
[name]	[number]

It was further resolved that the allottees be entered in the Register of Members as the holder of the shares specified in the second column opposite their names **and that** the relative share certificates be sealed and issued to the allottees.

3. Filing of returns

The Secretary produced to the Meeting the following returns for filing at the Companies Registry:

(a) Form No. 123 in respect of the increase in the authorized Share Capital;

(b) Form No. 88(2) in respect of the issue and allotment of [number] Ordinary Shares of £[value]each.

It was resolved that the forms be and are hereby approved **and that** the Secretary be and is hereby authorized and directed to sign each of them on behalf of the Company and to arrange for them to be filed at the Companies Registry.

....

[name]
CHAIRMAN

[NAME IN FULL] LIMITED

NOTICE IS HEREBY GIVEN that an Extraordinary General Meeting of the Company will be held at [address] on [date] at [time] at which the following Resolutions will be proposed as Ordinary Resolutions:

RESOLUTIONS

1. **That** the authorized Share Capital of the Company be increased to £[value] by the creation of [number] additional shares of £[value] each which shall be at the disposal of the directors who may allot or otherwise dispose of them or grant options over them to such persons (including any director) at such times and generally on such terms and conditions (subject to section 100, Companies Act 1985) as they think proper **and that** the authority conferred on the directors by this Resolution shall expire on the 5th anniversary of the passing of this Resolution but may be renewed, varied or extended by the Company in General Meeting from time to time.

2. **That** a sum of £[value] be capitalized out of the profit and loss account of the Company and applied in paying up in full at par, [number] unissued Shares of £[value] each in the Capital of the Company and that such Shares be appropriated to and distributed, credited as fully paid, among those persons who are registered at the close of business on [date] as the holders of existing Shares in the Capital of the Company in the proportion, as nearly as can be, of [number in words] new Shares for every [number in words] existing Shares held on that date, and that the Board be authorized and directed to appropriate the said sum of £[value] and issue the said [number] new Shares accordingly upon the terms that the new Shares shall rank *pari passu* in all respects with the existing issued Shares in the Company.

BY ORDER OF THE BOARD

....
[name]
[office held e.g. Secretary or Director or both]

Registered Office:
[address]

Dated: [date]

PROXIES
A member entitled to attend at the Meeting is entitled to appoint a proxy to attend and, on a poll, vote in his stead. A proxy need not be a member of the company.

[NAME IN FULL] LIMITED

MINUTES OF AN EXTRAORDINARY GENERAL MEETING

HELD AT [address]

ON [date] at [time]

PRESENT: [name] (In the Chair)
                [name]
                [name]
                [name]

1. A quorum being present and consent to short notice having been agreed the Meeting was duly constituted.
2. The Notice convening the Meeting was taken as read.
3. The Chairman proposed Resolution No. 1 which was put to the Meeting and declared carried.
4. The Chairman proposed Resolution No. 2 which was put to the Meeting and declared carried.
5. There being no other business to transact the Chairman declared the Meeting closed.

....

[name]
CHAIRMAN

[NAME IN FULL] LIMITED	No. [number]

The Companies Act 1985
Company Limited by Shares

ORDINARY RESOLUTIONS

(Passed [date])

At an Extraordinary General Meeting of the Company duly convened and held on [date] the following Resolutions were passed as Ordinary Resolutions:

RESOLUTIONS

1. **That** the authorized Share Capital of the Company be increased to £[value] by the creation of [number] additional shares of £[value] each which shall be at the disposal of the directors who may allot or otherwise dispose of them or grant options over them to such persons (including any director) at such times and generally on such terms and conditions (subject to section 100, Companies Act 1985) as they think proper **and that** the authority conferred on the directors by this Resolution shall expire on the 5th annivarsary of the passing of this Resolution but may be renewed, varied or extended by the Company in General Meeting from time to time.

2. **That** a sum of £[value] be capitalized out of the profit and loss account of the Company and applied in paying up in full at par, [number] unissued Shares of £[value] each in the Capital of the Company and that such Shares be appropriated to and distributed, credited as fully paid, among those persons who are registered at the close of business on [date] as the holders of existing Shares in the Capital of the Company in the proportion, as nearly as can be, of [number in words] new Shares for every [number in words] existing Shares held on that date, and that the Board be authorized and directed to appropriate the said sum of £[value] and issue the said [number] new Shares accordingly upon the terms that the new Shares shall rank *pari passu* in all respects with the existing issued Shares in the Company.

....
CHAIRMAN

P7. RIGHTS ISSUE

[NAME IN FULL] LIMITED

MINUTES OF A MEETING OF THE DIRECTORS

HELD AT [address]

ON [date] at [time]

PRESENT: [name] (In the Chair)
                [name]
                [name]
                [name]

1. Extraordinary General Meeting

It was resolved that an Extraordinary General Meeting be convened and held forthwith for the purpose of increasing the authorized Share Capital to £[value] in accordance with the Notice presented to the Meeting.

(The Meeting was then adjourned to allow the Extraordinary General Meeting to take place).

On reconvening, the Chairman reported that both the Resolutions proposed at the Extraordinary General Meeting had been passed unanimously.

2. Allotment of shares

It was resolved that [number] shares of £[value] each of the Company be issued for subscription at par to the shareholders appearing in the Register as at the close of business on [date] in the proportion of [number in words] new shares for every existing [number in words] shares held **and** that the Secretary be and is hereby authorized to issue provisional allotment letters to the said shareholders forthwith.

(The Meeting was then adjourned to enable the provisional allotment letters to be issued).

On reconvening at [time] there were produced to the meeting acceptances from each of the shareholders together with cheques for the subscription monies.

It was resolved that each of the shareholders be entered in the Register of members as the holder of the above mentioned shares **and** that the relative share certificates be [sealed and] issued.

3. Filing of returns

The Secretary produced to the Meeting the following returns for filing at the Companies Registry:
(a) Form No. 123 in respect of the increase in the authorized Share Capital;
(b) Form No. 88(2) in respect of the issue and allotment of [number] Shares of £[value] each.

It was resolved that the forms be and are hereby approved **and that** the Secretary be and is hereby authorized and directed to sign each of them on behalf of the Company and to arrange for them to be filed at the Companies Registry.

....
[name]
CHAIRMAN

[NAME IN FULL] LIMITED

NOTICE IS HEREBY GIVEN that an Extraordinary General Meeting of the Company will be held at [address] on [date] at [time] at which the following Resolutions will be proposed as an Ordinary Resolution:

RESOLUTION

That the authorized Share Capital of the Company be increased to £[value] by the creation of [number] additional shares of £[value] each which shall be at the disposal of the directors who may allot or otherwise dispose of them or grant options over them to such persons (including any director) at such times and generally on such terms and conditions (subject to section 100, Companies Act 1985) as they think proper **and that** the authority conferred on the directors by this Resolution shall expire on the 5th anniversary of the passing of this Resolution but may be renewed, varied or extended by the Company in General Meeting from time to time.

BY ORDER OF THE BOARD

....
[name]

[Office held, e.g. Secretary or Director or both]

Registered Office:
[address]

Dated: [date]

PROXIES

A member entitled to attend at the meeting is entitled to appoint a proxy to attend and, on a poll, vote in his/her stead. A proxy need not be a member of the company.

[NAME IN FULL] LIMITED

MINUTES OF AN EXTRAORDINARY GENERAL MEETING

HELD AT [address]

ON [date] at [time]

PRESENT: [name] (In the Chair)
             [name]
             [name]
             [name]

1. All members being present and consent to short notice being agreed the Meeting was duly constituted.

2. The Notice convening the Meeting was taken as read.

3. The Chairman proposed the Resolution relating to the increase in authorized Share Capital, which was put to the Meeting and declared carried.

4. There being no other business to transact the Chairman declared the Meeting closed.

....
[name]
CHAIRMAN

[NAME IN FULL] LIMITED	No. [number]

The Companies Act 1985
Company Limited by Shares

ORDINARY RESOLUTIONS

(Passed [date])

At an Extraordinary General Meeting of the Company duly convened and held on [date] the following Resolution was passed as an Ordinary Resolution:

RESOLUTION

THAT the authorized Share Capital of the Company be increased to £[value] by the creation of [number] additional shares of £[value] each which shall be at the disposal of the directors who may allot or otherwise dispose of them or grant options over them to such persons (including any director) at such times and generally on such terms and conditions (subject to section 100, Companies Act 1985) as they think proper **and that** the authority conferred on the directors by this Resolution shall expire on the 5th anniversary of the passing of this Resolution but may be renewed, varied or extended by the Company in General Meeting from time to time.

....
CHAIRMAN

[NAME IN FULL] LIMITED

RIGHTS ISSUE OF [number & class] SHARES OF £[value] EACH FULLY PAID ON [date].

To: [name]
      [address]

Dear Sir/Madam

PROVISIONAL LETTER OF ALLOTMENT

1. Pursuant to a Resolution of the Board of Directors passed on [date] you have been allotted, subject to the Memorandum and Articles of Association of the Company, [number & class] Shares of £[value] each being in the proportion of [number in words] new [class] Shares for every [number in words & class] Shares held at the close of business on [date].

2. The Shares so allotted rank pari passu in all respects with the existing Ordinary Shares of the Company.

3. If you wish to accept all the shares allotted to you, you should return this allotment letter, together with the amount payable £[amount], to [the Registered Office of the Company], [address]. Payment of the amount due will constitute acceptance of allotment. Cheques should be made payable to [name in full] Limited.

BY ORDER OF THE BOARD

....
[name]
[Office held, e.g. Secretary or Director or both]

Dated: [date]

P8. ANNUAL GENERAL MEETING

[NAME IN FULL] LIMITED

MINUTES OF A MEETING OF THE DIRECTORS

HELD AT [address]

ON [date]

PRESENT: [name] (In the Chair)
                  [name]
                  [name]
                  [name]

1. Financial statements

It was resolved that the Financial Statements for the period ended [date] including the dirctors' report be and they are hereby approved for submission to the forthcoming Annual General Meeting **and that** [name of director signing balance sheet] be and is hereby authorized to sign the balance sheet thereof and [secretary's name] the directors' report.

2. Annual General Meeting

It was resolved that the Annual General Meeting of the Company be convened at [address] on the [date in words, e.g. 'twelfth day of June 1990'] for the purpose of transacting the ordinary business of the Company in accordance with the terms of the Notice of the Annual General Meeting presented to the Meeting.

OR

It was resolved that the Annual General Meeting of the Company be convened forthwith in accordance with the Notice of the Annual General Meeting presented to the Meeting.

....

[name]
CHAIRMAN

NOTICE OF ANNUAL GENERAL MEETING (short form — private companies only)

| [NAME IN FULL] LIMITED |

NOTICE OF ANNUAL GENERAL MEETING

NOTICE IS HEREBY GIVEN that the [year] ANNUAL GENERAL MEETING of the Company will be held at [address] on [date] at [time] to transact the ordinary business of the Company.

BY ORDER OF THE BOARD

....
[name]
[office held, e.g. Secretary or Director or both]

Dated: [date]

Registered Office:
[address]

PROXIES

A member entitled to attend at the Meeting is entitled to appoint a proxy to attend and vote in his/her stead. A proxy need not be a member of the Company.

NOTICE OF ANNUAL GENERAL MEETING (long form)

[NAME IN FULL] LIMITED

NOTICE OF ANNUAL GENERAL MEETING

NOTICE IS HEREBY GIVEN that the [year] ANNUAL GENERAL MEETING of the Company will be held at [address] on [date] at [time] to transact the ordinary business of the Company, namely:

1. To receive the Financial Statements for the year ended [date] [and to declare a dividend].

2. To reappoint [name] a director of the Company.

3. To reappoint [name of firm] as auditors of the Company and to authorize the directors to fix their remuneration.

BY ORDER OF THE BOARD

....
[name]
[office held, e.g. Secretary or Director or both]

Dated: [date]

Registered Office:
[address]

PROXIES

A member entitled to attend at the Meeting is entitled to appoint a proxy to attend and vote in his/her stead. A proxy need not be a member of the Company.

[NAME IN FULL] LIMITED

MINUTES OF THE [YEAR] ANNUAL GENERAL MEETING OF THE COMPANY

HELD AT [address]

ON [date]

PRESENT: [name] (In the Chair)
                [name]
                [name]
                [name]

1. The Chairman reported that the consent of all members entitled to attend and vote at the Meeting had been obtained to the Meeting being held at short notice.

2. The Notice convening the Meeting and the Report of the Auditors on the Financial Statements for the period ended [date] were taken as read.

3. The Financial Statements of the Company for the period ended [date] were submitted to the Meeting and the Chairman proposed:

   That the Financial Statements of the Company for the period ended [date] together with the Directors' and Auditors' Reports thereon be and they are hereby received, approved and adopted.

   The Resolution was put to the Meeting and declared carried.

4. The Chairman proposed:

   That the following Directors who retire from the Board in accordance with the Articles of Associations be and are hereby re-elected.

   [name]
   [name]

   The Resolution was put to the Meeting and declared carried.

5. The Chairman proposed:

   That the Auditors, Messrs [name], be and are hereby reappointed until the conclusion of the next General Meeting at which Financial Statements are laid before the Company and that their remuneration be fixed by the Board of Directors.

   The Resolution was put to the Meeting and declared carried.

6. There being no other business the Chairman declared the Meeting closed.

....
[name]
CHAIRMAN

P9. ANNUAL GENERAL MEETING (full agenda)

[NAME IN FULL] LIMITED

ANNUAL GENERAL MEETING

[time], [date]

AGENDA

1 Notice of meeting and auditors' report

Chairman: 'It is now [time], the appointed time for the Meeting to commence and, as a quorum is present, we will start.'

'I will now ask for the Notice convening the Meeting and the Auditors' Report to be read.'

Secretary [name]: To read Notice.*

Auditors [name]: To read Report.*

2 Directors' report

Chairman: 'May I presume that you will agree to the Directors' Report being taken as read.'

3 Chairman's statement (if applicable)

Chairman: 'I do not propose adding to the statement which is on page [number] of the accounts, but will deal with any question when we consider the accounts. I therefore suggest we move straight on to the Directors' Report and Financial Statements.'

*This does not need to be read but it is customary.

4 Directors' report and accounts

Chairman:	'I will now ask for a proposer that the Directors' Report and Financial Statements for the period ended [date] be 'adopted and received and that a final dividend of [amount] pence per Ordinary Share of £1 be declared payable on [date] to the holders of such shares as at [date]].'
[name]	'I propose that the Directors' Report and the Financial Statements for the period ended [date] be and are hereby adopted and received.'
Chairman:	'I will ask for a seconder for that motion.'
[name]	'I hereby second the motion.'
Chairman:	'Before I put the motion to the vote, I shall be glad to answer any questions on the Report or on the Financial Statements.'
After questions	
Chairman:	'I will now put the motion to the vote: Those in favour
	....
	Those against
	....
	I declare the motion carried.'

5 Election of directors (if applicable)

Chairman:	'There are two directors who come up for re-election by rotation and I will deal with each election in turn. It is the turn of [name] to retire and, being eligible, he/she offers him/herself for re-election. I will, therefore, ask for a proposer for the motion.'
[name]	'I propose that [name] be and is hereby re-elected a director of the Company.'

Chairman:	'I will ask for a seconder for the motion.'
[name]	'I hereby second the motion.'
Chairman:	'I will now put the motion to the vote:
	Those in favour
	....
	Those against
	....
	I declare the motion carried.'
	'It is also the turn of [name] to retire and, being eligible, he/she offers him/herself for re-election. I will, therefore, ask for a proposer for the motion.'
[name]	'I propose that [name] be and is hereby re-elected a Director of the Company.'
Chairman:	'I will now ask for a seconder for the motion.'
[name]	'I hereby second the motion.'
Chairman:	'I will now put the motion to the vote:
	Those in favour
	....
	Those against
	....
	I declare the motion carried.'

6 Reappointment of auditors

Chairman:	'Under the Companies Act 1985 it is necessary to reappoint our auditors each year. Messrs [name] have indicated their willingness to continue in office and I therefore propose that they be re-appointed auditors to the conclusion of the next general meeting at which financial statements are laid before the Company.
	Is there a seconder?'

[name]	'I hereby second the motion.'
Chairman:	'I will now put the motion to the vote: Those in favour
	....
	Those against
	....
	I hereby declare the motion carried.'

7 Auditors' remuneration

Chairman:	'I now propose that the remuneration of the auditors be fixed by the Directors. Is there a seconder?'
[name]	'I hereby second the motion.'
Chairman:	'I will now put the motion to the vote: Those in favour
	....
	Those against
	....
	I hereby declare the motion carried.'

8 Closure

Chairman:	'I now declare the meeting closed.'

P10. ANNUAL GENERAL MEETING (TO BE ADJOURNED)

[NAME IN FULL] LIMITED

MINUTES OF A MEETING OF THE DIRECTORS

HELD AT [address]

ON [date]

PRESENT: [name] (In the Chair)
             [name]
             [name]
             [name]

1. Financial statements

The Chairman reported that the Financial Statements of the Company for the year to [date] were not yet available. However, to fulfil the requirements of the Companies Act 1985, it was necessary to hold the [year] Annual General Meeting of the Company by [date, not being more than 15 months from previous AGM].

2. Annual General Meeting

It was resolved that the [year] Annual General Meeting of the Company be convened and held immediately following the close of this Meeting.

....
[name]
CHAIRMAN

[NAME IN FULL] LIMITED

MINUTES OF THE [year] ANNUAL GENERAL MEETING OF THE COMPANY

HELD AT [address]

ON [date]

PRESENT: [name] (In the Chair)
             [name]
             [name]
             [name]

1. The Chairman reported that the consent of all members entitled to attend and vote at the Meeting had been obtained to the Meeting being held at short notice.

2. The Chairman reported that the Financial Statements for the year to [date] were not yet available and proposed:

    That the Meeting be and is hereby adjourned until such time as the Financial Statements are available.

    The Resolution was put to the Meeting and declared carried.

3. There being no other business the Chairman declared the Meeting closed.

....
[name]
CHAIRMAN

P11. ANNUAL GENERAL MEETING (RECONVENING)

[NAME IN FULL] LIMITED

MINUTES OF A MEETING OF THE DIRECTORS

HELD AT [address]

ON [date]

PRESENT: [name] (In the Chair)
                   [name]
                   [name]
                   [name]

1. Financial statements

It was resolved that the Financial Statements for the period ended [date] including the directors' report be and are hereby approved for submission to the forthcoming Annual General Meeting **and that** [name of director signing balance sheet] be and is hereby authorized to sign the balance sheet thereof.

2. Annual General Meeting

It was resolved that the Adjourned [year, could be different for year in which meeting is held] Annual General Meeting of the Company be reconvened forthwith in accordance with the Notice of the Annual General Meeting presented to the Meeting.

....

[name]
CHAIRMAN

[NAME IN FULL] LIMITED

NOTICE OF ADJOURNED ANNUAL GENERAL MEETING

Notice is hereby given that the ADJOURNED [year] ANNUAL GENERAL MEETING of the Company will be reconvened at [address] on [date] at [time] to transact the ordinary business of the Company.

BY ORDER OF THE BOARD

....
[name]
[office held, e.g. Secretary or Director or both]

Dated: [date]

Registered Office:
[address]

PROXIES

A member entitled to attend at the Meeting is entitled to appoint a proxy to attend and vote in his/her stead. A proxy need not be a member of the Company.

[NAME IN FULL] LIMITED

MINUTES OF THE ADJOURNED [year] ANNUAL GENERAL MEETING OF THE COMPANY

HELD AT [address]

ON [date]

PRESENT: [name] (In the Chair)
[name]
[name]
[name]

1. The Chairman reported that the consent of all members entitled to attend and vote at the Meeting had been obtained to the Meeting being held at short notice.

2. The Notice convening the Meeting and the Report of the Auditors on the Financial Statements for the period ended [date] were taken as read.

3. The Financial Statements of the Company for the period ended [date] were submitted to the Meeting and the Chairman proposed:

   That the Financial Statements of the Company for the period ended [date] together with the Directors' and Auditors' Reports thereon be and they are hereby received, approved and adopted.

   The Resolution was put to the Meeting and declared carried.

4. The Chairman proposed:

   That the following Directors who retire from the Board in accordance with the Articles of Association be and are hereby re-elected.
   [name]
   [name]
   The Resolution was put to the Meeting and declared carried.

5. The Chairman proposed:

   That the Auditors, Messrs [name], be and are hereby reappointed until the conclusion of the next General Meeting at which Financial Statements are laid before the Company and that their remuneration be fixed by the Board of Directors.

   The Resolution was put to the Meeting and declared carried.

6. There being no other business the Chairman declared the Meeting closed.

....
[name]
CHAIRMAN

P12. CONSENT TO SHORT NOTICE AND AGREEMENT TO ACCEPT FINANCIAL STATEMENTS

[NAME IN FULL] LIMITED

We the undersigned, together holding all the Shares giving the right to attend and vote at the Annual General Meeting convened for [date] at [time] at [address] hereby

(a) consent to the convening of the said Meeting for the day and place above mentioned for the purposes set forth notwithstanding that less than twenty-one days' notice thereof shall have been given; and

(b) agree that copies of the documents required to be sent to us in accordance with section 238 of the Companies Act 1985, not later than twenty-one days before the date of the said Meeting shall be deemed to have been duly sent notwithstanding that they are sent less than twenty-one days before the date of the Meeting.

Dated: [date]

....
[name]

....
[name]

....
[name]

....
[name]

CONSENT TO SHORT NOTICE

[NAME IN FULL] LIMITED

We, the undersigned, holding [all/not less than 95% of] the Shares giving the right to attend and vote at the [Annual/Extraordinary] General Meeting convened for [date] at [time] at [address] hereby consent to the convening of the said Meeting for the day and place above mentioned for the purposes set forth notwithstanding that less than [fourteen/twenty-one] days' notice thereof shall have been given

Dated: [date]

....
[name]

....
[name]

....
[name]

....
[name]

P13. FORM OF PROXY (simple)

[NAME IN FULL] LIMITED

I/We, [name] of [address] a member(s) of the above named company, hereby appoint the chairman of the meeting (see note 1 below) as my/our proxy to attend and vote on my/our behalf at the [Annual/Extraordinary] General Meeting of the Company to be held on [date] and at any adjournment thereof.

Dated: [date]

....
[name]/[For and on half of]

NOTES

1. A member may appoint a proxy of his/her own choice. If such an appointment is made, delete the words 'the chairman of the meeting' and insert the name of the person appointed proxy in the space provided.

2. If the appointor is a corporation, this form must be under its common seal or under the hand of some officer or attorney duly authorized in that behalf.

3. In the case of joint holders, the signature of any one holder will be sufficient, but the names of all the joint holders should be stated.

4. To be valid, this form must be completed and deposited at [address] not less than 48 hours before the time fixed for holding the meeting or adjourned meeting.

FORM OF PROXY (with voting directions)

[NAME IN FULL] LIMITED

I/We, [name] of [address] a member(s) of the above named company, hereby appoint the chairman of the meeting (see note 1 below) as my/our proxy to attend and vote on my/our behalf at the [Annual/Extraordinary] General Meeting of the Company to be held on [date] and at any adjournment thereof.

Dated: [date]

....

[name]/[For and on half of]

Please indicate with an X in the spaced below how you wish your votes to be cast.

	FOR	AGAINST
RESOLUTION 1 [To receive the [year] accounts]		
RESOLUTION 2 [To reappoint [name] a director]		
RESOLUTION 3 [To reappoint Messrs [name] as auditors and to authorize the directors to fix their remuneration]		

NOTES

1. A member may appoint a proxy of his/her own choice. If such an appointment is made, delete the words 'the chairman of the meeting' and insert the name of the person appointed proxy in the space provided.
2. If the appointor is a corporation, this form must be under its common seal or under the hand of some officer or attorney duly authorized in that behalf.
3. In the case of joint holders, the signature of any one holder will be sufficient, but the names of all the joint holders should be stated.
4. If this form is returned without any indication as to how the person appointed proxy shall vote, he/she will exercise his/her discretion as to how he/she votes or whether he/she abstains from voting.
5. To be valid, this form must be completed and deposited at [address] not less than 48 hours before the time fixed for holding the meeting or adjourned meeting.

P14. APPOINTMENT OF A REPRESENTATIVE

[NAME IN FULL] LIMITED

MINUTES OF A MEETING OF THE DIRECTORS

HELD AT [ADDRESS]

ON [date] at [time]

PRESENT: [name] [In the Chair)
                [name]
                [name]
                [name]

Appointment of representative

It was resolved that [name] be appointed the company's representative, pursuant to section 375, Companies Act 1985, to attend the [Annual/Extraordinary] General Meeting of [name of company] to be held on [date] and at any adjournment of that meeting [AND that the [name] be and is authorized to sign a form of consent to such meeting being held at short notice].

....
[name]
CHAIRMAN

[ON COMPANY HEADED NOTEPAPER]

The Director   [date]
[Name in full] Limited
[Address]

Dear Sirs

We confirm that [name] has been appointed by this Company as its representative, pursuant to section 375, Companies Act 1985, to attend the [Annual/Extraordinary] General Meeting of your company to be held on [date] and at any adjournment of that meeting.

[We also confirm that the above mentioned person is authorized to sign on behalf of this company a form of consent to such meeting being held at short notice].

Yours faithfully

For and on behalf of
[Company name]

P15. REMOVAL OF A DIRECTOR

A. Special Notice to remove a Director

The Directors
[name]

I hereby give notice, pursuant to sections 303 and 379, Companies Act 1985, of my intention to propose the following resolution as an ordinary resolution at the [next annual/extraordinary] general meeting of the company [to be held on [date]].

Resolution

that [name] be removed from his/her office of director of the company.

....
[name]
[Address]
[Date]

B. Notice to be given by the Company to Director to be Removed

Included in the notice of the [Annual/Extraordinary] General meeting will be the following item of business —

To consider the following resolution which will be proposed as an ordinary resolution, special notice having been given pursuant to sections 303 and 379, Companies Act 1985.

Resolution

That [name] be removed from his/her office of director of the company.

P16. ALTERNATE DIRECTORS

A. Form of Appointment of Alternate Director

Pursuant to Article [number] of the articles of association of [name] Limited and subject to the approval of [a majority of] the directors, I, [name], being a director of [name] Limited, hereby appoint [name], of [address], to be my alternate director.

....
[name]
[Address]
[Date]

B. Form of Revocation of Appointment of Alternate Director

Pursuant to Article [number] of the articles of association of [name] Limited, I, [name], hereby revoke the appointment dated [date] of [address] as my alternate director of [name] Limited.

....
[name]
[Address]
[Date]

C. Directors' Resolution approving Appointment of Alternate Director

There was produced a form of appointment dated [date] by which [name] appoints [name] to be his/her alternate director.

Resolved that the appointment by [name] of [name] to be his/her alternate director be approved.

D. Directors' Minute noting Revocation of Appointment of Alternate Director

A form of revocation dated [date] by which [name] revokes the appointment of [name] as his/her alternate director was produced and noted.

P17. REMOVAL OF AUDITORS

A. Resolution for Removal of Auditors (in general meeting)

That [name] be removed from office as auditors of the company with immediate effect [and that [name] be appointed auditors of the company in their place to hold office until the conclusion of the next general meeting at which accounts are laid before the company and that their remuneration be fixed by the directors].

B. Resolution for Appointment of Auditors other than retiring Auditors (in general meeting)

That [name] be appointed auditors of the company in place of the retiring auditors to hold office until the conclusion of the next general meeting at which accounts are laid before the company and that their remuneration be fixed by the directors.

C. Form of Special Notice

The Directors   [date]
[name]

I give notice under sections 379 and 391A, Companies Act 1985, of my intention to move the following ordinary resolution at the [next Annual/Extraordinary] General meeting of the company [to be held [date]]:

Resolution
[Text of appropriate resolution, e.g. A or B above.]

………………………………………………
[name]
[address]
[date]

D. Notice of Relevant General Meeting

The notice of the relevant general meeting should make reference to receipt of the special notice, e.g.:

To consider the following resolution, special notice having been received of the intention to propose the resolution as an ordinary resolution:

Resolution

[Text of resolution.]

P18. INTERIM DIVIDEND

[NAME IN FULL] LIMITED

MINUTES OF A MEETING OF THE DIRECTORS

HELD AT [address]

ON [date]

PRESENT: [name] (In the Chair)
                                   [name]
                                   [name]
                                   [name]

INTERIM DIVIDEND

That an interim dividend for the year ended [date] of £[value] per share on the [class] shares of £[value] each of the Company be declared payable on [date] to shareholders registered at the close of business on [date].

....

[name]
CHAIRMAN

[NAME IN FULL] LIMITED

Registered in England No: [number]

Registered Office: [address]

TO:
[name]
[address]

TAX VOUCHER

[class] Shares of £[value] each.

Interim dividend of £[value] per share in respect of the year ended [date].

Payment date: [date]

I certify that advance Corporation Tax of an amount equal to that shown below as tax credit will be accounted for to the Collector of Taxes. **This voucher should be kept**. It will be accepted by the Inland Revenue as evidence of tax credit in respect of which you may be entitled to claim payment or relief.

....
[name]
SECRETARY

Dated: [date]

Number of [class] Shares of £[value] each	Tax Credit	Dividend
[number]	£[value]	£[value]

P19. FINAL DIVIDEND

[NAME IN FULL] LIMITED

MINUTES OF A MEETING OF THE DIRECTORS

HELD AT [address]

ON [date]

PRESENT: [name] (In the Chair)
                [name]
                [name]
                [name]

FINAL DIVIDEND

Having regard to the financial statements for the year ended [date] it was resolved to recommend to the members of a final dividend of £[value] per share on the [class] shares at £[value] each of the Company AND THAT an Extraordinary General Meeting be convened and held forthwith for the purpose of declaring the said final dividend in accordance with the Notice presented to the Meeting.

....
[name]
CHAIRMAN

141

[NAME IN FULL] LIMITED

NOTICE IS HEREBY GIVEN that an Extraordinary General Meeting of the Company will be held at [address] on [date] at [time] for the purpose of declaring a final dividend in respect of the year ended [date].

BY ORDER OF THE BOARD

....
[name]
SECRETARY

Dated: [date]

Registered Office:
[address]

PROXIES

A member entitled to attend at the Meeting is entitled to appoint a proxy to attend and, on a poll, vote in his/her stead. A proxy need not be a member of the Company.

[NAME IN FULL] LIMITED

MINUTES OF AN EXTRAORDINARY GENERAL MEETING

HELD AT [address]

ON [date]

PRESENT: [name] (In the Chair)
             [name]
             [name]
             [name]

1. A quorum being present and consent to short notice having been agreed the Meeting was duly constituted.

2. The Notice convening the Meeting was taken as read.

3. The Chairman proposed:

   That a final dividend for the year ended [date] of £[value] per share on the [class] shares of £[value] each of the Company be declared payable [date] to shareholders registered at the close of business on [date].

   The Chairman put the resolution to the vote and declared it carried.

4. There being no other business to transact the Chairman declared the Meeting closed.

....
[name]
CHAIRMAN

[NAME IN FULL] LIMITED

Registered in England No: [number]

Registered Office: [address]

TO:
[name]
[address]

TAX VOUCHER

[class] Shares of £[value] each.

Final dividend of £[value] per share in respect of the year ended [date].

Payment date: [date]

I certify that advance Corporation Tax of an amount equal to that shown below as tax credit will be accounted for to the Collector of Taxes. **This voucher should be kept**. It will be accepted by the Inland Revenue as evidence of tax credit in respect of which you may be entitled to claim payment or relief.

....
[name]
SECRETARY

Dated: [date]

Number of
[class] Shares
of £[value] each   Tax Credit   Dividend

[number]   £[value]   £[value]

P20. WAIVER AND RELEASE OF DIVIDEND

I, [name in full] of [address], the Registered Holder of [number] Ordinary Shares of £[value] each, numbered [number] to [number], in the capital of [NAME IN FULL] LIMITED (hereinafter called the Company) **hereby**

(i) Waive all right to participate by reason of my said Ordinary Shares in all dividends whether interim, final or otherwise declared by the Company or the Directors thereof, and

(ii) Release unto the Company such sums as would have been payable from time to time by way of dividend relative to my said Ordinary Shares.

Such waiver and release to apply to all dividends declared as aforesaid before such time as I revoke this waiver by notice in writing to the Company at its Registered Office provided that such dividends shall be declared and become payable withn 12 months of the date hereof.

DATED: [date]

Signed Sealed and Delivered
by the said

....
[name in full]

In the presence of:

....
[name]

P21. WAIVER OF PRE-EMPTION RIGHTS

[NAME IN FULL] LIMITED

Written Resolutions of all the members for the time being of the Company pursuant to section 381A, Companies Act 1985.

We, the undersigned, being the holders of the entire issued share capital of [name in full] **resolve:**

1. **That** notwithstanding the provisions of the Articles of Association of the Company regulating the transfer of shares, we hereby consent and agree to the undermentioned transfers of shares of the Company and hereby authorize and empower the Directors of the Company to register such transfers lodged with the Company for registration in connection with such transfers:

Transferor	Transferee	Number of Shares
[name]	[name]	[number]
[name]	[name]	[number]

2. **That** the provisions of Article [number] of the Articles of Association of the Company be and are hereby waived in respect of such transfers.

Dated: [date]

....
[name]

....
[name]

....
[name]

....
[name]

....
[name]

....
[name]

P22. DECLARATION OF TRUST FOR NOMINEE SHARE

I, [name in full] of [address], **HEREBY DECLARE** that the one Share of £[value] in the capital of [NAME IN FULL] LIMITED (hereinafter called 'the Company') whose registered office is situated at [address], which is registered in my name in the books of the Company, are held by me **UPON TRUST** for [name of beneficial owner in full] (hereinafter called 'the Beneficial Owner') of/whose registered office is situate at [address] and I hereby agree to transfer pay deal with and exercise such Share and all dividends interest and other rights which may accrue to me by virtue thereof in such manner and only in such manner as the Beneficial Owner may from time to time direct and I agree to notify the Beneficial Owner of any and all matters affecting the said Share which may come to my attention or notice and to carry out the instructions of the Beneficial owner with regard thereto.

I have handed to the Beneficial Owner a transfer in blank in respect of such Share and I hereby authorize the Beneficial Owner to complete and date the transfer when he so desires.

DATED: [date]

Signed Sealed and Delivered
by the said

[name in full]

In the presence of:

....
[name]

P23. INDEMNITY FOR LOST CERTIFICATE

To the Directors of [name] LIMITED

The original certificate(s) of title relating to the undermentioned securities of the above-named Company has/have been lost or destroyed.

Neither the securities nor the certificate(s) of title thereto have been transferred, charged, lent or deposited or dealt with in any manner affecting the absolute title thereto and the person(s) named in the said certificate(s) is/are the person(s) entitled to be on the register in respect of such securities.

I/We request you to issue a duplicate certificate(s) of title for such securities and in consideration of your doing so, undertake (jointly and severally) to indemnify you and the Company against all claims and demands (and any expenses thereof) which may be made against you or the Company in consequence of your complying with this request and of the Company permitting at any time hereafter a transfer of the said securities, or any part thereof, without the production of the said original certificate(s).

I/We undertake to deliver to the Company for cancellation the said original certificate(s) should the same ever be recovered.

PARTICULARS OF CERTIFICATE(S) LOST OR DESTROYED

Particulars of Certificate	Amount and Class of Securities	In favour of

Dated: [date]

Signature(s) ....

P24. ELECTIVE RESOLUTION

[NAME IN FULL] LIMITED

Written Resolution of all the Members for the time being of the Company pursuant to section 381A, Companies Act 1985.

Resolved that, pursuant to section 379A, Companies Act 1985, the Company hereby elects:

(a) to dispense with the laying of accounts and reports before the company in general meetings in accordance with section 252, Companies Act 1985;

(b) to dispense with the holding of Annual General Meetings in accordance with section 366A, Companies Act 1985:

(c) to dispense with the obligation to appoint auditors annually in accordance with section 386, Companies Act 1985;

(d) that the provisions of section 80A, Companies Act 1985, shall apply instead of the provisions be sections 80(4) and (5);* and

(e) to reduce the majority required for the holding of a general meeting (other than Annual General Meetings) and the passing of a special resolution at short notice to 90% in accordance with sections 369(4) and 378(3), Companies Act 1985 as amended by section 115(3), Companies Act 1989.

Dated: [date]

....
[name]

....
[name]

....
[name]

....
[name]

* This paragraph may be used in conjunction with a resolution to give the relevant authority to the directors.

No. [number]

The Companies Act 1985
Company Limited by Shares

WRITTEN RESOLUTION

of

[NAME IN FULL] LIMITED

By a written resolution, pursuant to section 381A, Companies Act 1985, signed by or on behalf of all the members of the Company entitled to attend and vote at general meetings and dated [date], the following Elective Resolution was duly adopted:

RESOLUTION

That, pursuant to section 379A, Companies Act 1985, the Company hereby elects:

(a) to dispense with the laying of accounts and reports before the company in general meetings in accordance with section 252, Companies Act 1985;

(b) to dispense with the holding of Annual General Meetings in accordance with section 366A, Companies Act 1985;

(c) to dispense with the obligation to appoint auditors annually in accordance with section 386, Companies Act 1985;

(d) that the provisions of section 80A, Companies Act 1985, shall apply instead of the provisions of sections 80(4) and (5);* and

(e) to reduce the majority required for the holding of a general meeting (other than Annual General Meetings) and the passing of the special resolution at short notice to 90% in accordance with sections 369(4) and 378(3), Companies Act 1985 as amended by section 115(3), Companies Act 1989.

....
DIRECTOR

* This paragraph may be used in conjunction with a resolution to give the relevant authority to the directors.

P25. ELECTIVE RESOLUTION — revocation

[NAME IN FULL] LIMITED

Written Resolution of all the Members for the time being of the Company pursuant to section 381A, Companies Act 1985.

Resolved that, pursuant to section 379A (3), Companies Act 1985, the elective Resolution adopted on [date] is hereby revoked.

Dated: [date]

....
[name]

....
[name]

....
[name]

....
[name]

No. [number]

The Companies Act 1985
Company Limited by Shares

WRITTEN RESOLUTION

of

[NAME IN FULL] LIMITED

By a Written Resolution, pursuant to section 381A, Companies Act 1985, signed by or on behalf of all the members of the Company entitled to attend and vote at general meetings and dated [date], the following Resolution was duly adopted:

RESOLUTION

That, pursuant to section 379A (3), Companies Act 1985, the elective Resolution adopted on [date] is hereby revoked.

....
[name]
DIRECTOR

P26. RE-REGISTRATION AS A PUBLIC COMPANY

[NAME IN FULL] LIMITED

MINUTES OF A MEETING OF THE DIRECTORS

HELD AT [address]

ON [date] at [time]

PRESENT: [name] (In the Chair)
               [name]
               [name]
               [name]

1. Re-registration as a public company

It was resolved that

(i) the Company be re-registered as a public company;

(ii) [name], subject to the required resolutions being passed in General Meeting, be authorized and directed to complete a statutory declaration pursuant to section 43, Companies Act 1985, and make the appropriate application to the Registrar of Companies.

2. Extraordinary General Meeting

It was resolved that an Extraordinary General Meeting be convened and held forthwith for the purpose of re-registering the Company as a public company and amending the Memorandum and Articles of Association of the Company, in accordance with the Notice presented to the Meeting.

....
CHAIRMAN

[NAME IN FULL] LIMITED

NOTICE IS HEREBY GIVEN that an Extraordinary General Meeting of the Company will be held at [address] on [date] at [time] at which the Resolution below will be proposed as a Special Resolution:

RESOLUTION

That pursuant to the provisions of section 43, Companies Act 1985, the Company be re-registered as a public company and that the memorandum of association of the Company be thereupon altered as follows:

(a) by deleting the existing clause 1 and substituting therefore the following clauses to be number 1 and 2:

'1 The name of the Company is [name, to include plc or public limited company].

2 The Company is to be a public company'; and

(b) by renumbering the existing clauses 2, 3, 4 and 5 as clauses 3, 4, 5 and 6 respectively;

*[and that thereupon the regulations contained in the document marked 'A' submitted to this meeting and, for the purpose of identification, signed by the chairman hereof be approved and adopted as the Articles of Association of the company in substitution for, and to the exclusion of all the existing articles thereof.]

BY ORDER OF THE BOARD

....
[name]

[office held, e.g. Secretary or Director or both]

Dated: [date]

Registered Office:
[address]

PROXIES
A member entitled to attend at the Meeting is entitled to appoint a proxy to attend and, on a poll, vote in his stead. A proxy need not be a member of the company.

* Only required if new articles are to be adopted.

[NAME IN FULL] LIMITED

MINUTES OF AN EXTRAORDINARY GENERAL MEETING

HELD AT [address]

ON [date] at [time]

PRESENT: [name] (In the Chair)
                     [name]
                     [name]
                     [name]

1. A quorum being present and consent to short notice having been agreed the Meeting was duly constituted.

2. The Notice convening the Meeting was taken as read.

3. The Chairman proposed the Resolution set out in the Notice, which was put to the Meeting and declared carried as a Special Resolution.

4. There being no other business to transact the Chairman declared the Meeting closed.

....
[name]
CHAIRMAN

No. [number]

The Companies Act 1985
Company Limited by Shares

SPECIAL RESOLUTION

of

[NAME IN FULL] LIMITED

(Passed [date])

At an Extraordinary General Meeting of the Company duly convened and held on [date] the following Resolution was passed as a Special Resolution:

RESOLUTION

That, pursuant to the provisions of section 43, Companies Act 1985, the Company be re-registered as a public company and that the Memorandum of Association of the Company be thereupon altered as follows:

(a) by deleting the existing clause 1 and substituting therefore the following clauses to be number 1 and 2:

'1 The name of the Company is [name, to include plc or public limited company].
2 The Company is to be a public company'; and

(b) by renumbering the existing clauses 2, 3, 4 and 5 as clauses 3, 4, 5 and 6 respectively;

[and that thereupon the regulations contained in the document marked 'A' submitted to this meeting and, for the purpose of identification, signed by the chairman hereof be approved and adopted as the Articles of Association of the company in substitution for, and to the exclusion of all the existing articles thereof.]

....
CHAIRMAN

P27. REPURCHASE OF SHARES

[NAME IN FULL] LIMITED

MINUTES OF A MEETING OF THE DIRECTORS

HELD AT [address]

ON [date]

PRESENT: [name] (In the Chair)
             [name]
             [name]
             [name]

Re-purchase of shares

(i) Proposed Contract

There was presented to the Meeting a draft of the proposed contract between [name of shareholder] and the Company for the purchase by the Company out of distributable profits of the [number and class] Shares at £[value] each beneficially owned and held by [name of shareholder] for a consideration of [amount].

It was resolved that the terms of the said agreement be and are hereby approved and that, subject to the passing of the required resolution(s), [name of a director] be and is hereby authorized to sign the agreement on behalf of the Company.

(ii) Members' Resolution(s)

It was resolved that the Secretary arrange for the Members to approve the resolution(s), [to amend the Articles of Association to provide for the re-purchase of shares and], to approve the agreement to re-purchase [name of shareholder] shares.

(The Meeting then adjourned to enable the Resolutions to be signed.)

On reconvening, the Chairman reported that the Members' Resolution(s) had been signed.

(iii) Completion

It was resolved that the contract for the re-purchase be completed on [date].

(iv) Filing of Return

There was presented to the Meeting Form No. 169 in respect of the company purchasing its own shares for filing at the Companies Registry.

It was resolved that the form be and is hereby approved and that the Secretary be and is hereby authorized and directed to sign it on behalf of the Company and to arrange for it to be filed at Companies House.

....

[name]
CHAIRMAN

[NAME IN FULL] LIMITED

Written Resolution of all the Members for the time being of the Company pursuant to section 381A, Companies Act 1985.

RESOLVED

*[1. **That** the Articles of Association of the Company be amended by the insertion of the following new article immediately following the existing article [number]:

'[number]A Subject to the provisions of the Companies Act 1985, the company may purchase its own shares (including any redeemable shares) and, if it is a private company, make a payment in respect of the redemption or purchase of its own shares otherwise than out of distributable profits of the Company or the proceeds of a fresh issue of shares.']

2. **That** the off-market purchase of shares in the capital of the Company on the terms of the proposed contract to be made between the Company and the [name of shareholder] as annexed to [these/this] Resolution(s) be and is hereby approved.

Dated: [date]

....
[name]

....
[name]

....
[name]

....
[name]

* This resolution is only required if the relevant provision is not already in the company's articles.

No. [number]

The Companies Act 1985
Company Limited by Shares

WRITTEN RESOLUTION

of

[NAME IN FULL] LIMITED

By Written Resolutions, pursuant to section 381A, Companies Act 1985, signed by or on behalf of all the members of the Company entitled to attend and vote at general meetings and dated [date], the following Resolutions were duly adopted:

RESOLUTIONS

[1. **That** the Articles of Association of the Company be amended by the insertion of the following new article immediately following the existing article [number]:

'[number]A Subject to the provisions of the Companies Act 1985, the company may purchase its own shares (including any redeemable shares) and, if it is a private company, make a payment in respect of the redemption or purchase of its own shares otherwise than out of distributable profits of the Company or the proceeds of a fresh issue of shares.']

2. **That** the off-market purchase of shares of the capital of the Company on the terms of the proposed contract to be made between the Company and the [name of shareholder] as annexed to [these/this] Resolution(s) be and is hereby approved.

....
[name]
DIRECTOR

'Proposed contract'

THIS AGREEMENT is made the [date] day of [month] 19[year]

BETWEEN

1. [name and address of shareholder] (hereinafter called 'the Vendor')
   and
2. [NAME IN FULL] LIMITED whose registered office is situated at [address] (hereinafter called 'the Company')

WHEREAS

A. The Company was incorporated in England on [date] under the Companies Act(s) [year(s)], and has an authorized share capital of £[value] divided into [number and class] shares of £[value] each all of which are in issue and are fully paid [amend as appropriate].

B. The Vendor is the beneficial owner of [number and class] shares of £[value] each in the capital of the Company.

C. This Agreement is made by the Company pursuant to Part V of the Companies Act 1985 and by Article [number] of the Articles of Association of the Company.

D. The terms of this Agreement were authorized by a Written Resolution of the Company adopted on [date].

NOW IT IS HEREBY AGREED as follows:

1. The Vendor shall sell and the Company shall purchase [number and class] shares of £[value] each in the Company, which shares are free from all charges, liens, encumbrances and claims.

2. The total purchase price for the shares shall be £[amount] payable in cash on completion.

3. Completion shall take place on [date] at [address].

   whereupon:

   (a) the Vendor shall deliver to the Company for cancellation the share certificate(s) in respect of the number of shares sold under this Agreement or in the case of lost certificates such indemnity as the Company may reasonably require.

   (b) the Company shall deliver to the Vendor a cheque in the sum of £[amount] pursuant to Clause 2 of this Agreement.

4. Time shall be of the essence of this Agreement.

5. (a) This Agreement constitutes the whole agreement between the parties hereto and no variation shall be effective unless made in writing.

(b) This Agreement shall be governed by the law of England.

IN WITNESS whereof the parties have executed this Agreement the day and year first above written.

Signed by [name of shareholder] ....

Signed by [name of director]..
for and on behalf of
[NAME IN FULL] LIMITED

P28. REPURCHASE OF SHARES (OUT OF CAPITAL)

[NAME IN FULL] LIMITED

MINUTES OF A MEETING OF THE DIRECTORS

HELD AT [address]

ON [date]

PRESENT: [name] (In the Chair)
                     [name]
                     [name]
                     [name]

Re-purchase of shares

(i) Proposed Contract

There was presented to the Meeting a draft of the proposed contract between [name of shareholder] and the Company for the purchase by the Company out of capital of the [number and class] Shares at £[value] each beneficially owned and held by [name of shareholder] for a consideration of £[amount].

It was resolved that the terms of the said agreement be and are hereby approved and that, subject to the passing of the required resolutions and the fulfilling of the other provisions of sections 171 to 177, Companies Act 1985, [name of a director] be and is hereby authorized to sign the agreement on behalf of the Company.

(ii) Statutory Declaration and Audit Report

The Meeting carefully considered the terms of a statutory declaration required in connection with the re-purchase of shares out of capital. The Meeting was satisfied that immediately following the re-purchase there would be no grounds on which the Company could be found unable to pay its debts nor would it impinge on their ability to pay its debts as and when they fell due during the ensuing year.

There was presented to the Meeting a report from the auditors for annexing to the statutory declaration stating that:

(a) they had enquired into the Company's state of affairs;
(b) the amount specified in the declaration as the permissible capital payment for the shares in question was in their view properly determined in accordance with sections 171 to 175, Companies Act 1985; and
(c) they are not aware of anything to indicate that the opinion expressed by the directors in the declaration was unreasonable in the circumstances.

It was resolved that the terms of the statutory declaration be agreed and approved and that the same be declared before a solicitor.

(The Meeting then adjourned to enable the declaration to be completed.)

On reconvening, the Chairman reported that the statutory declaration had been completed.

(iii) Members' Resolutions

It was resolved that the Secretary arrange for the Members to approve the resolutions, [to amend the Articles of Association to provide for the re-purchase of shares], to approve the agreement to re-purchase [name of shareholder] shares and to approve the payment out of capital.

....
[name]
CHAIRMAN

[NAME IN FULL] LIMITED

Written Resolutions of all the Members for the time being of the Company pursuant to section 381A, Companies Act 1985.

RESOLVED

*[1. **That** the Articles of Association of the Company be amended by the insertion of the following new article immediately following the existing article [number]:

   '[number]A Subject to the provisions of the Companies Act 1985, the company may purchase its own shares (including any redeemable shares) and, if it is a private company, make a payment in respect of the redemption or purchase of its own shares otherwise than out of distributable profits of the Company or the proceeds of a fresh issue of shares.']

2. **That** the off-market purchase of shares in the capital of the Company on the terms of the proposed contract to be made between the Company and the [name of shareholder] as annexed to these Resolutions be and is hereby approved.

3. **That** the payment of £[amount] out of capital of the Company as defined in sections 171 to 172 of the Companies Act 1985 in respect of the purchase of [name and class] Shares of £[value] each from the [name of shareholder] be authorized and approved.

Dated: [date]

....
[name]

....
[name]

....
[name]

....
[name]

* This resolution is only required if the relevant provision is not already in the company's articles.

No. [number]

The Companies Act 1985
Company Limited by Shares

WRITTEN RESOLUTION

of

[NAME IN FULL] LIMITED

By a written resolution, pursuant to section 381A, Companies Act 1985, signed by or on behalf of all the members of the Company entitled to attend and vote at general meetings and dated [date], the following Written Resolutions were duly adopted:

RESOLUTION

[1. **That** the Articles of Association of the Company be amended by the insertion of the following new article immediately following the existing article [number]:

'[number]A Subject to the provisions of the Companies Act 1985, the company may purchase its own shares (including any redeemable shares) and, if it is a private company, make a payment in respect of the redemption or purchase of its own shares otherwise than out of distributable profits of the Company or the proceeds of a fresh issue of shares.']

2. **That** the off-market purchase of shares in the capital of the Company on the terms of the proposed contract to be made between the Company and the [name of shareholder] as annexed to these Resolutions be and is hereby approved.

3. **That** the payment of £[amount] of a capital of the Company as defined in sections 171 to 172 of the Companies Act 1985 in respect of the purchase of [number and class] Shares of £[value] each from the [name of shareholder] be authorized and approved.

....
[name]
DIRECTOR

For *London Gazette*

[NAME IN FULL] LIMITED	No. [number]

NOTICE is hereby given that:

By a Written Resolution of the above Company pursuant to section 381A, Companies Act 1985 adopted on [date], the payment of £[amount] was authorized out of the capital of the Company in respect of the purchase by the Company of [number and class] shares of £[value] each from [name of shareholder] The amount of the permissible capital payment was £[amount].

The statutory declaration and auditor's report dated [date] are available for inspection at [address], the registered office of the Company.

Any creditor of the Company may apply to the High Court pursuant to section 176 of the Companies Act 1985 within five weeks immediately following the date of the aforementioned Resolution, [date] for an Order prohibiting the payment.

Signature: ....
                [name]
Description: CHAIRMAN

Authenticated* for insertion in the *London Gazette* by

.... of [address]

* Authentication should be made by a Solicitor, a member of a recognized body of Accountants or a Chartered Secretary.

For national newspaper

[NAME IN FULL] LIMITED	No. [number]

NOTICE is hereby given that:

By a Written Resolution of the above Company pursuant to section 381A, Companies Act 1985 adopted on [date], the payment of £[amount] was authorized out of the capital of the Company in respect of the purchase by the Company of [number and class] shares of £[value] each from [name of shareholder] The amount of the permissible capital payment was £[amount].

The statutory declaration and auditor's report dated [date] are available for inspection at [address], the registered office of the Company.

Any creditor of the Company may apply to the High Court pursuant to section 176 of the Companies Act 1985 within five weeks immediately following the date of the aforementioned Resolution, [date] for an Order prohibiting the payment.

Signature: ....
                    [name]
Description: CHAIRMAN

[NAME IN FULL] LIMITED

MINUTES OF A MEETING OF THE DIRECTORS

HELD AT [address]

ON [date]

PRESENT: [name] (In the Chair)
               [name]
               [name]
               [name]

Re-purchase of shares

(i) Completion

Further to the Board Meeting held on [date] and the Members' Resolutions passed that day, there having been no objections raised to the re-purchase of shares **it was resolved** that the contract for the re-purchase of shares be concluded and **that** the completion date be the [date].

(ii) Filing of Return

The Secretary produced to the Meeting Form No. 169 in respect of the company purchasing its own shares.

It was resolved that the form be and is hereby approved and that the Secretary be and is hereby authorized and directed to sign it on behalf of the Company and to arrange for it to be filed at the Companies Registry.

....
[name]
CHAIRMAN

P29. FINANCIAL ASSISTANCE

[NAME IN FULL] LIMITED

MINUTES OF A MEETING OF THE DIRECTORS

HELD AT [address]

ON [date]

PRESENT: [name] (In the Chair)
               [name]
               [name]
               [name]

Financial assistance for the purchase of shares

(i) The Assistance

The Chairman reported to the Meeting the terms of proposed Financial Assistance to [name of beneficiary] by the Company to enable [name of beneficiary] to purchase [number and class] shares at £[value] each in the Company by [detail of Assistance].

It was resolved that the terms of the said Financial Assistance be and are hereby approved subject to the passing of the required resolution and the fulfilling of the other provisions of sections 155 to 158, Companies Act 1985.

(ii) Statutory Declaration and Audit Report

The Meeting carefully considered the terms of a statutory declaration required in connection with the provision of Financial Assistance to [name of beneficiary]. The Meeting was satisfied that immediately following the provision of the Financial Assistance there would be no grounds on which the Company could be found unable to pay its debts nor would it impinge on their ability to pay its debts as and when they fell due during the ensuing year.

There was presented to the Meeting a report from the auditors for annexing to the statutory declaration stating that:

(a) they had enquired into the Company's state of affairs; and
(b) they are not aware of anything to indicate that the opinion expressed by the directors in the declaration was unreasonable in the circumstances.

It was resolved that the terms of the statutory declaration be agreed and approved and that the same be declared before a solicitor.

(The Meeting then adjourned to enable the declaration to be completed.)

On reconvening, the Chairman reported that the statutory declaration had been completed.

(iii) Members' Resolution

It was resolved that the Secretary arrange for the Members to adopt the required resolution to authorize the provision of Financial Assistance to [name of beneficiary].

....

[name]
CHAIRMAN

[NAME IN FULL] LIMITED

Written Resolution of all the Members for the time being of the Company pursuant to section 381A, Companies Act 1985.

RESOLVED

That the provision by the Company of Financial Assistance to [name of beneficiary] for the purpose of acquiring [number and class] Shares of £[value] in the capital of the Company be and is hereby approved.

Dated: [date]

....
[name]   [name]

....
[name]   [name]

No. [number]

The Companies Act 1985
Company Limited by Shares

WRITTEN RESOLUTION

of

[NAME IN FULL] LIMITED

By a Written Resolution, pursuant to section 381A, Companies Act 1985, signed by or on behalf of all the members of the Company entitled to attend and vote at general meetings and dated [date], the following Resolution was duly adopted:

RESOLUTION

That the provision by the Company of Financial Assistance to [name of beneficiary] for the purpose of acquiring [number and class] Shares of £[value] in the capital of the Company be and is hereby approved.

....
[name]
DIRECTOR

P30. DORMANT COMPANIES — NON-APPOINTMENT OF AUDITORS

[NAME IN FULL] LIMITED

MINUTES OF A MEETING OF THE DIRECTORS

HELD AT [address]

ON [date]

PRESENT: [name] (In the Chair)
              [name]
              [name]
              [name]

Extraordinary General Meeting

It was resolved that an Extraordinary General Meeting of the Company be convened forthwith for the purpose of not appointing Auditors in accordance with section 252 of the Companies Act 1985.

....
[name]
CHAIRMAN

[NAME IN FULL] LIMITED

NOTICE OF EXTRAORDINARY GENERAL MEETING

NOTICE IS HEREBY GIVEN that an Extraordinary General Meeting of the Company will be held at [address] on [date] at [time] at which* the following Resolution will be proposed as a Special Resolution:

That, pursuant to Section 250 Companies Act 1985, auditors shall not be appointed.

BY ORDER OF THE BOARD

....

[name]
[office held, e.g. Secretary or Director or both]

Dated: [date]

Registered Office:
[address]

PROXIES

A member entitled to attend at the Meeting is entitled to appoint a proxy to attend and, on a poll, vote in his/her stead. A proxy need not be a member of the Company.

* If the last audited accounts need to be presented to the members add in the words 'the audited financial statements for the period ended [date] will be presented and'

[NAME IN FULL] LIMITED

MINUTES OF AN EXTRAORDINARY GENERAL MEETING

HELD AT [address]

ON [date]

PRESENT: [name] (In the Chair)
[name]
[name]
[name]

1. The Chairman reported that the consent of all members entitled to attend and vote at the Meeting had been obtained to the Meeting being held at short notice.

2. The notice convening the Meeting [and the Report of the Auditors on the Financial Statements for the period ended [date] were] **was taken as read.**

[3. The financial statements of the Company for the period ended [date] were submitted to the Meeting and the Chairman proposed:

   That the financial statements of the Company for the period ended [date] together with the Directors' and Auditors' Reports thereon be and they are hereby received.

   The Resolution was put to the Meeting and declared carried.]

4. The Chairman proposed:

   That, pursuant to Section 250 Companies Act 1985, auditors shall not be appointed.

   The Resolution was put to the Meeting and declared carried as a Special Resolution.

5. There being no other business the Chairman declared the Meeting closed.

....

[name]
CHAIRMAN

No. [number]

The Companies Act 1985
Company Limited by Shares

SPECIAL RESOLUTION

of

[NAME IN FULL] LIMITED

(Passed [date])

At an Extraordinary General Meeting of the Company duly convened and held on [date] the following Resolution was passed as a Special Resolution:

RESOLUTION

That, pursuant to section 250 of the Companies Act 1985, auditors shall not be appointed.

....
[name]
CHAIRMAN

P31. DORMANT ACCOUNTS

[NAME IN FULL] LIMITED	No. [number]
Balance Sheet at [date]	

19[year] and 19[year]
£

ASSETS

Cash in Hand   [value]

FINANCED BY:
Called Up Share Capital (see note)   [value]

The Company has remained dormant within the meaning of section 250 of the Companies Act 1985 throughout the financial period ended [date]

APPROVED BY THE BOARD ON [date]
(and signed on its behalf)

....
[name]
DIRECTOR

NOTE TO THE ACCOUNTS

£

SHARE CAPITAL

CALLED UP SHARE CAPITAL
   Ordinary Shares of £ 1 each   [value]
AUTHORIZED
   Ordinary Shares of £ 1 each   [value]

Index

_____